A Matter of Luck

A Matter of Luck

Published by
Barzipan Publishing
www.barzipan.com

© James M Killeen 2014

ISBN: 978-0-9573792-6-8
Kindle edition ISBN: 978-0-9573792-7-5

James M Killeen asserts his moral right to be identified as the author of this book.

Designed by
Kitty Carruthers

Printed and bound
Short Run Press
25 Bittern Road
Sowton Industrial Estate
Exeter
Devon EX2 7LW

CIP Data: A catalogue record for this book is available from the British Library.

All rights reserved. No part of this publication may be reproduced, stored in a retrieval system, or transmitted in any form or by any means, electronic, mechanical, photocopying, recording, or otherwise, without the prior permission of the copyright owners.

A Matter of Luck

James M Killeen

Barzipan Publishing
not what you'd expect

Contents

Introduction 7

Chapter 1 : Luck – Fact or Fiction? 9

Chapter 2 : Luck and Cause and Effect 19
    Determinism 22
    Destiny 25
    The Butterfly Effect 26

Chapter 3 : Magic and Luck 29
    Taboos 37
    Ordeals 41

Chapter 4 : Philosophy, Religion and Luck 45
    Philosophy 46
    Religion 48
    Luck in the Bible 50
    Lutheranism 52
    Calvinism 53
    Judaism 55
    Islam 55
    Hinduism 57
    Reincarnation 57
    Divine Providence 59

Chapter 5 : Probability and Luck 61
    Optimum Strategy 72
    Newcomb's Paradox 74
    Game Theory 76
    Odds 80
    Gambling 82
    Randomness 83

Murphy's Law	85
The Man Who Broke the Bank at Monte Carlo	87
Aleatory	91

Chapter 6: Luck and Coincidence — 95
Remarkable Coincidences — 99
Synchronicity — 101
Serendipity — 103
Collective Unconscious — 108
Akashic Record — 109

Chapter 7: Luck and Related Phenomena — 113
Astrology — 114
Fortune-telling — 116
Premonitions — 120
Precognition — 123
Intuition — 124
Superstition — 126
Miracles — 129
Feng Shui — 132
Auspices and Omens — 134
Oracles — 136
The Fates — 139
The Muses — 139
Hubris — 141
Numerology — 147
The Big Bang — 149
Rare Earth Hypothesis — 156
The Placebo Effect — 162
Biorhythm — 163
Lucky/Unlucky people — 165

Chapter 8: Luck: How to Improve It — 171
Maslow's Hierarchy of Needs — 175

References and Further Reading — 181

Introduction

Sometimes when you look at the world around you and see how things are proceeding, it is easy to feel confused, helpless or angry. There can be a feeling that things are out of control, not just on a personal level, but on every other level as well. You are swept along by the cares, joys and monotony of everyday life, blown in different directions by conflicting desires, while all the time thinking that things could be better. When a broader view is taken and a person looks beyond their beautiful little planet into the vastness of space, the feeling of helplessness is magnified. There is the realisation of being merely an insignificant being on a little planet on the edge of the Milky Way, which in turn is just a tiny galaxy in the vastness of the millions of galaxies in the universe. You draw back from this feeling of insignificance. You console yourself with thoughts of your uniqueness, your individuality, your place in society, your little successes, and may even experience a little warm glow of self-importance, a feeling which, sadly, does not last very long for most people. Soon the doubts, questions and insecurities reappear

You see around you a world which, in many ways, does not satisfy your idea of 'fair'. You see people whose lives are blackened by poverty, illness or despair. You notice others who appear to have more than their share of the good things in life. You look for an explanation as to why some suffer and some prosper. Of course, there are some people who 'bring it on themselves', but not all. Why is it, you ask, that the best efforts of some lead to nought, while others achieve success effortlessly? The rake abuses his body but dies of old age and the clean living, early-to-bed-early-to-rise man drops dead of a heart attack at 45. It just doesn't make sense. Well, maybe it's all down to genetics, intelligence, or mental attitude. Or, perhaps, it is all just a matter of luck.

There are numerous quotations affirming or denying the role of luck in life. Opinions range from 'Life is what you make it' to Forrest Gump's 'Life is like a box of chocolates' and 'Luck is everything'. So, you tell yourself, it is all down to luck – but then the thought quickly comes that this is a cop-out, an excuse for failure and lack of effort. Better to face reality and admit that people should take the blame or credit for what they are. You think of the 'self-made' man who never tires of telling people about his humble beginnings and how hard work got him where he is – but then there is also the other successful person who puts some, or a large part, of his success down to luck

Clearly, there are cases where reckless or unhealthy lifestyles lead to early death, where lack of success is attributable to lack of effort and where hard work brings success, but this is not the whole story. There are also the occasions when recklessness leads to longevity, lack of effort to success and hard work to failure. Living does not seem to be an exact science.

Neither is the study of luck. It is not possible to 'prove beyond a reasonable doubt' that luck does or does not exist. The best one can do is look at luck and try to see if there is some rational, religious or magical evidence that might prove or disprove its existence. Even after all that, it may come down to a 'gut feeling' and 'I believe' or 'I don't believe'.

Life does not seem to provide a level playing field. With our inbuilt senses of fairness and justice, we search for an explanation, or justification, for this. Scientists tell us that it is all just cause and effect and that this simple law can explain everything that happens. Were you to consider all the causes and effects that made you what you are – a unique individual, living where you are, doing what you are doing in the early part of the 21st century – you might be tempted to ask a few 'What if…' questions. With just tiny variations in the cause and effect chain that made you what you are, you could be a completely different person, or not exist at all. And how far back do you have to follow this chain? Determinists tell us that the laws governing the universe are fixed and that everything that happens was determined billions of years ago at the time of the birth of the universe. From that first cause, all else follows and continues to follow in the present and into the future, and there does not seem to be anything we can do about it. How much of life is under our control and how much is just a matter of luck? Each individual must choose the answer that seems best.

Chapter 1

Luck – Fact or Fiction?

Everything in life is luck.
Donald Trump

I'm a great believer in luck and I find the harder I work, the more I have of it.
Thomas Jefferson

We must believe in luck, for how else can we explain the success of those we don't like.
Jean Cocteau

Life is not a spectacle or a feast – it is a predicament.
George Santayana

A very unlikely thing happened to Maureen Wilcox in June 1980. She chose the winning numbers for both the Massachusetts and Rhode Island lotteries. Unfortunately for her, the numbers she chose for the Rhode Island lottery were the winning numbers for the Massachusetts lottery, and vice versa. On the face of it she would appear to have been very unlucky and lost one, if not two, lottery prizes. Looked at in another way, all she had lost was the cost of the lottery tickets. But, somehow, that does not seem to be a sufficient answer.

So, what was happening here? Was Maureen Wilcox experiencing some kind of hugely improbable outcome, the victim of what Shakespeare called 'outrageous fortune'? Did fortune have anything to do with it, or was it just 'one of those things'? And, if it was fortune, what was that, where did it come from and, perhaps more pertinently, does it really exist?

There are many ways of looking at luck. First, there are those who deny its very existence. They say that it is just a superstition, believed in by those who do not understand the theory of probability or how to apply logical thinking to situations. Were we to know about those things, they say, we would never believe in anything so 'unscientific' as luck. Consequently, to the rationalist, luck is just ignorance arising from primitive, pre-logical thought patterns. He will also accuse believers in luck of not being familiar with the concept of cause and effect and point out that just because B follows A doesn't necessarily mean that it was caused by A, that your recent win at poker was not caused by a rabbit's foot that you happened to have in your pocket or because you were wearing your 'lucky' underwear. He will no doubt add that this type of fallacious thinking is the same as saying that, because it began to rain as you left your house, the act of leaving your house caused the rain to start falling. Yes, to the rationalist, there is no such thing as luck. But, tell that to a gambler who has just flipped a coin five times and each time it has come up heads. He just knows that the next toss will also turn up heads because the coin is 'on a roll', just like the gambler. Another gambler might take the completely opposite view. As the coin has just come up heads five times in succession, tails is due. He is feeling lucky and just knows the coin will come up tails. There would be little point in telling either of them that the coin does not have a memory and that each flip is totally independent and unrelated to the one that comes before it or will come after it. They refuse to accept that random events are unpredictable. The odds on the next toss of the coin being a head or a tail are 50–50. If you toss a coin a million times, then the theory of probability tells us that it will come up heads and tails roughly half a million times. That does not mean that every alternate toss will be heads and then tails. There may be long runs of heads or tails, but eventually it will even out. On one level, the gambler may know all this, but it is too prosaic and banal for him. He believes in luck and just knows the next toss will end up heads. If the coin does come up heads it will consolidate his belief in luck, but if tails comes up he will not abandon his belief. He will tell you that 'lady luck' can be fickle and you cannot be lucky all the time.

Could it be that belief in luck is just a cop-out for losers? Rather than attribute their failures in life to stupidity, lack of effort or recklessness, they put them down to 'bad luck'. In this way, they absolve themselves of responsibility for all the bad things that happen to them, as it is all luck and, consequently, outside their control. It is just plain bad luck and they lament that, were it not for their bad luck, they would have no luck at all.

But then what about people who believe that they are lucky? Is this another way of not accepting responsibility or, in this case, credit, for what happens to them? Is it just a display of false modesty to ward off any jealousy or envy that their success might arouse?

Perhaps it is all in the mind, the product of the beliefs, hopes, expectations and disappointments that go to make up the individual, or might it be some kind of self-fulfilling prophesy? Some who consider themselves unlucky will waste time bemoaning their ill fortune, become negative, depressed, angry, frustrated or fatalistic and give up trying to improve their lot by their own efforts. Sunk in negativity, they are not receptive to opportunities that cross their paths. On the other hand, those who consider themselves lucky are likely to be more positive and confident. They approach life in a more optimistic way, thus increasing their chances of success. Maybe belief in good or bad luck is just a state of mind and has nothing to do with the reality of the great world outside.

But what, you may ask, about people who seem to have bad things always happening to them? The rationalist would tell us that everyone will experience a certain amount of good and bad in the course of their lives and it has nothing to do with luck, good or bad. It is just a matter of probability, of things that are likely to happen in the course of a lifetime. A person who has been involved in a serious car accident will often be described as having been 'unlucky' but then, if he has escaped serious injury, will be called 'lucky'. So, which is he – lucky or unlucky – or neutral, or do they cancel each other out? Seldom will anyone point out the thousands of miles of accident-free driving that he has enjoyed down the years. Did he have good luck during all these years and miles and now has this one piece of bad luck, which was surely due, based on probability? Has he been lucky overall, and should he be seen as such? It is more probable that the longer you drive the more likely it is that you will have an accident. Fortunately, most accidents are quite minor and will give rise to comments such as, 'He was lucky' or 'It could have been worse'. To complicate matters further, there is the 'blessing in disguise'. The driver of the other car, who happens to be an attractive and unmarried woman, was uninjured and visits the man in hospital. Her initial feelings of guilt mixed with pity blossoms into love and they end up getting married and living happily ever after. Now, we ask again, was the accident lucky or unlucky?

The story is told of a poor farmer and his son who eked out a meagre existence on a small farm. Their most valuable possession was a horse. One morning, the farmer went to fetch his horse, but could not find it. For two days, they looked for the horse, but without success. That evening, a neighbouring, more prosperous farmer, stopped by for a visit. He commiserated with the farmer.

'That was bad luck losing your horse like that. What will you do when it comes time for ploughing and sowing? Truly, you have had very bad luck.'

'We do not know what is for good or ill in this life,' replied the poor farmer philosophically.

The following day the farmer's horse returned, and with it was a fine young mare. The neighbour was quick to notice this and came to congratulate the farmer on his good fortune.

'Now you have two horses and yesterday you had none. Truly, you have been blessed by good fortune.'

'We do not know what is for good or ill in this life,' replied the poor farmer.

Two days later, the farmer's son tried to ride the young mare but was thrown and sustained a broken leg. Along came the neighbour.

'Now that your son has a broken leg, he will not be able to assist you with the farm work and you will not be able to make a living. Truly, you have been unfortunate.'

'We do not know what is for good or ill in this life,' replied the farmer.

A week later, an army recruiting officer knocked on the poor farmer's door, demanding that his son present himself for military service. The son hobbled to the door and when the officer saw his condition, he went on his way,

The next knock on the door was the visiting neighbour.

'It was lucky that your son had a broken leg or he would have been taken away by the army and maybe sent to war and killed or who knows what. Truly, he is lucky to have a broken leg.'

'We do not know what is for good or ill in this life,' replied the poor farmer.

And so on.

So, what is luck? Luck can be defined as events that happen or do not happen, which are beyond, or appear to be beyond, the control of the individual. If we look for a reason or explanation, we will be unlikely to find one. We see around us some people for whom everything in life seems to go smoothly and others for whom everything is a struggle. We may try to rationalise this and put this success or failure down to the talents and efforts of the individuals involved. But, somehow, that does not seem to be a satisfactory answer. As stated earlier, intelligence, hard work and persistence do not always guarantee success, nor their absence failure. We rationalise that there must be something else to explain this, something beyond all these human qualities, in an attempt to find an explanation for why things happen the way they do. This is where luck comes in. We say that some are lucky, others are unlucky, that's the way it is – and leave it at that.

Whether we call it superstition, fallacious thinking, faulty logic, failure to understand the connection between cause and effect or a genuine force of nature, there is one thing of which we can be certain. There are hundreds of millions of people in the world today who believe in luck. Man has believed in luck since the dawn of history, and probably before. In view of this, it might be interesting to look a little deeper and try to determine whether good or bad luck really exist and, if they do, why one person should be favoured and another cursed. And, beyond that, if luck is a force in the world, is there anything a person who believes he or she is unlucky can do to improve their luck? In this context, it might help with our enquiries were we to divide luck into different types and see how each affects, or appears to affect, individuals.

The first type of luck deals with things that a person is powerless to change or influence. A person's place and time of birth, his parentage and upbringing, are powerful and formative factors in his life that are beyond his control. One man is born into a poor family in a depressed neighbourhood and his genetic make-up predisposes him to cancer or heart problems, while another finds herself in a rich family in a leafy suburb and her genetic make-up is such that she is likely to live into her nineties. It is difficult to resist the temptation of saying the former was unlucky and the latter lucky. This kind of luck is sometimes called constitutional luck.

A second type of luck relates to haphazard, random or chance events that occur. Being run down by a drunk driver or being 'in the wrong place at the wrong time' would be examples of this type of luck. Being struck by lightning, contracting a rare disease, winning the lottery or being selected as the one-millionth customer in a supermarket and showered with gifts, would be further examples. Of course, sometimes we forget that *not* being struck by lightning, *not* contracting a rare disease or *not* being run down by a drunk driver could also be regarded as lucky. The person who is struck by lightning is counted extremely unlucky but, as in the case of the car accident, if he is not killed, is counted 'lucky to survive'. This is similar to the earlier case of good luck following on bad luck and seeming to cancel each other out, but the man struck by lightning might look at it in another way. There are also differences. With the first type of luck, circumstances are completely outside the control of the individual while, with the second, there might have been something the individual could have done to avoid the bad things that happened or attract the good things, like the lottery or supermarket successes. For example, during a lightning storm, a person is advised to take every precaution to avoid being struck by going to what would be considered a safe place and avoiding dangerous places, like under a tree or near metal objects. To avoid illness, a person can be immunised against every disease for which there is a vaccine, eat healthy food, avoid people who are ill and never travel to places where certain illness are endemic. Even if one were to take all possible precautions, there would still be a chance of being hit by lightning or contracting a disease. All the measures taken might not be enough to avoid the results of randomness, chance or luck.

A third type of luck is known as moral luck. Bernard Williams and Thomas Nagel did pioneering work in this field and wrote incisively on its implications. They considered the implications if morality were subject to, or influenced by, luck. Every person of sound mind who has reached the use of reason is deemed responsible for his or her actions and omissions. So, if a person does something wrong or is guilty of not doing something which they should have, we feel that it is only fair and just that he or she should suffer the consequences. This is particularly so when it seems that the individual could reasonably have foreseen what his actions or omissions were likely to lead. In that case, we would say they were completely to blame. On the other hand, we are likely to be less harsh in our judgement if it appears that the individual were coerced or frightened into doing something, the action was performed by accident or the individual had not foreseen the consequences of his actions or negligence. In a court case involving the death of a person, it would be the difference between murder and manslaughter. Generally speaking, a person will be punished according to how culpable he was judged to be in a given situation.

But it may not be that simple. This is shown when we consider a type of luck which has been called resultant moral luck. Those who have considered this issue sometimes illustrate the dilemma involved with the following story. Two drivers, A and B, are driving along a city street. Driver A goes through a red light just as an old lady is crossing the street. He does everything possible to avoid hitting her but knocks her down and kills her. Driver B also runs a red light but does not kill anyone, getting away with a traffic ticket. An impartial observer would be likely to say that Driver A is morally more to blame than Driver B as his actions have caused a death. However, Driver B was equally culpable in failing to stop at the red light. The main difference between the two drivers' circumstances was that, in the case of Driver A, an event occurred over which he had no control; the old lady crossing the street. A similar event did not occur to Driver B when he ran the red light. Had Driver B been faced with the same situation as Driver A, the result would likely have been the same. There is no difference in what either of them could have done. Despite all this, we are likely to be stronger in condemning and blaming Driver A.

This presents a moral difficulty. Generally speaking, a person should be held morally responsible only for what he performed or neglected to perform. In this context, both drivers should be equally blameworthy. This answer, however, does not satisfy our sense of justice. Although the actions of Drivers A and B were similar, the consequences were different. But the difference was not caused by the drivers, but by the old lady who happened to be crossing the street when Driver A failed to stop at the red light. So, is morality right or wrong, just a matter of chance, of luck? How different would the situation be if both drivers were drunk, or at least above the legal blood alcohol limit?

Constitutive moral luck relates to the personal characteristics of a person. Each individual is different due to variations in genetic make-up, intelligence, temperament, upbringing, environment and education. These factors will influence a person's actions. So, should the same level of moral blame apply to all people? In one way, it seems unjust to apply the same standard to all individuals – but then, all are equal before the law and there cannot be different rules for every person. It is known that a very high proportion of prisoners in jails in Europe, the US and other parts of the world are autistic or have some other type of mental deficiency and, therefore, have a different ways of looking at the world than 'normal' people. They may be more likely to commit crimes, especially if not given special-needs intervention when young. Should allowances be made for this predisposition to criminality and socially unacceptable behaviour? The justice system does try to compensate by taking into consideration mitigating or extenuating circumstances and, like the Mikado, 'make the punishment fit the crime', but even this does not always render what most people would regard as justice.

Every normal individual is considered as having free will and, therefore, being responsible for his actions, but there are occasions when a person's actions are determined by events outside his control. Even though a person has free will, there are times when there will be restrictions on his choices. The question then arises whether he should be held responsible for those actions. In addition, there are cases where a person is faced with what has been called 'the devil's alternative', when the choice is not between good and bad but between two bad situations. This aspect of moral luck is called causal moral luck.

Circumstantial moral luck deals with the various situations in which the individual finds himself. Consider the differences in circumstances of someone living in Pol Pot's Cambodia with that of a person living in a civilised, well-run democracy. Their environments are very different and they will be faced with very different choices. For the most part, it was just a matter of luck where they happened to find themselves, and not everyone can pack up and leave when they find themselves in an undesirable place. Should both individuals be subject to the same moral and ethical judgements? There have been cases where individuals in dire circumstances have resorted to extreme measures, such as cannibalism. The will to live is very strong and, in an emergency, will override many niceties of morality. While we would regard cannibalism as disgusting, we would have to concede that there might be circumstances in which it might be morally justifiable.

There are two sides to the issue of moral luck. If one accepts that it exists, then how, and to what extent, does this affect the degree of moral culpability of the individual? If a person's actions are determined by his innate characteristics, then are his actions voluntary, or is there a predisposition to certain types of behaviour? Were one to accept that moral luck exists, then there is the problem of determining the level of individual responsibility involved. If, on the other hand, one refuses to believe in moral luck or concede that it has any influence in situations, then it should not be a consideration in determining the ethics of an action or its moral status. In this view, a person is completely responsible for all his actions and all the consequences of these actions, foreseen or not. This would apply whether or not the action was completely voluntary or if it had been impossible to have foreseen all its repercussions.

Attempts have been made, particularly by the philosopher Susan Wolf, to find a middle ground between these two positions. Wolf came up with the idea of a rationalist and irrationalist position. From the rationalist's point of view, both Driver A and Driver B are equally blameworthy. Both did wrong in running the red light and it should not matter that one was unlucky while the other was lucky. Both were at fault and responsible for the outcomes, albeit they were different. In this view, moral blame relates to actions rather than their results. The irrational viewpoint would not blame Driver B as much as Driver A, as the level of blame is related to the consequences of the action. Wolf attempts to reconcile the two viewpoints by postulating what she calls a 'virtuous agent', who would accept that he could not separate himself from the consequences of his actions. Drivers A and B should not feel the same, even though they were both equally wrong, because the outcomes were different. Morally and ethically, the driver who killed the old woman should feel more guilty than the driver who, luckily, got away with a traffic ticket. This appears to be a satisfactory resolution to the problem and appeals to our senses of justice and fair play. But then, does luck have anything to do with justice or fair play?

Chapter 2

Luck and Cause and Effect

Shallow men believe in luck. Strong men believe in cause and effect.
Ralph Waldo Emerson

If one does not know to which port they are sailing, no wind is favourable.
Seneca

Fortune brings in some boats that are not steered.
William Shakespeare, *Cymbeline*, Act IV, Scene iii

Causality is the relationship between cause and effect and postulates that an event (called a cause) and a second event (called the effect) are related because the second event happens because of the first. For example, if you bang your finger with a hammer, then the result is a sore finger, the cause being the blow of the hammer. It is just that simple. Or is it?

Let's look at the cause. Why did the hammer hit your finger? Maybe you were distracted, or the light was bad, or you are just not very good with a hammer, or you slipped, or were hung-over from the night before. Were one of these to have contributed to your sore finger, then it was also part of the cause. We could go even further back. Why were you disturbed? Why did you slip? Why were you hung-over? You might say that you were hung-over because you had a fight with your wife, stormed out of the house, went to the bar, drank too much and felt terrible the following day when you were trying to repair the wooden fence outside your house.

Now let us look at the effect. The pain may be just the beginning of it. The initial pain caused you to scream and use obscene language. You have to take time off work to go for an x-ray. Your finger needs to be bandaged and you are so clumsy as a result that you drop your mobile phone and, later, cut yourself while shaving. (In the insurance business, this is known as progressive damage.) It was all the result of hitting your finger with a hammer. So maybe cause and effect are not as simple as they first appear.

Consider the following case. A shoots B dead. Therefore, A is the cause of B's death. Agreed, but there are other causes too. Without a gun and bullet, A could not have shot B. So, the manufacturers of the gun and bullet are also partly the cause of B's death. What about those who dug the ore out of the ground, or those who refined and transported it to the weapons and ammunition factories? They also must surely be also part of the cause. And you could go right back to the man who first discovered how to produce iron from ore and even further back to the formation of the iron mine from which the ore was obtained. Without just one of them, A would not have been able to shoot B. Perhaps, even B himself was part of the cause. Had he done or said something that had caused A to become murderous? If B had never been born, then A could not have killed him, so now part of the cause must be B's ancestors. The chain could stretch right back to Adam. In fact, as we shall see later, there are those who claim that everything that happens today can be traced back to the beginning of the universe. However, it is very unlikely that A will be able to claim any of these in mitigation at his murder trial, unless he has a particularly slick lawyer.

And this applies not only to people. If every natural event is the result of some previous cause, then again we must go back to the beginning of the universe to find the original cause. The events that caused effects that were in turn the causes of other effects are an unbroken chain back to the beginning of time and space, to the Big Bang, to God. But what about the first cause? What was this the result of? What caused the first cause? This is known as the 'cosmological argument' or 'first cause', and for those who deny God and the Bible's version of creation, it presents a conundrum similar to the question of the chicken and the egg.

But what has all this got to do with luck? The rationalist will tell us that were we to fully understand cause and effect, we would have no reason to look to luck as an explanation of events which appear fortunate or unfortunate, as everything that happened had a cause and was not the result of some mysterious force that operated for good or evil, favouring some over others for some inexplicable reason. According to the rationalist, what people regarded as good or bad luck had perfectly reasonable and logical explanations. Therefore, there was no such thing as luck – just cause and effect.

Man has been trying to understand cause and effect for thousands of years. Aristotle was not the first to consider the question, but he is probably one of the best known. Aristotle, to put it simply, saw causes as the answers to the question 'why?' and he divided them into four types. The first type he called the material cause, that from which a thing is made, such as a chair being made from wood or a gun from metal. The formal cause related to the form or shape of an object, or what the object is intended to be. The efficient cause is the entity or agent that makes the change. The final cause is the reason something is done or exists.

Let's take the example of Mr X who wins $1 million in a lottery. People who have not won, and lament their own lack of good fortune, will describe him as lucky. Now, let us look more closely at Mr X's win. He picked a set of numbers that were entered in the computer where he purchased his ticket. So, at least he went to the trouble and expense of buying a ticket, whereas many of those who did not win may not have gone to that trouble or expense. Now Mr X was in with a chance with the millions of others who had also purchased tickets for the lottery. The moment for the draw arrives, the machine is turned on, the balls whirl and bounce in the glass dome and one drops out. In succession, a number of others drop out until six or seven or whatever number are out. The balls that are out have the same numbers as are on Mr X's ticket and he wins. What are the chances of that? The chances (probability) of that depend on the number of balls in the drum and the number that a gambler has to correctly select. If there are fifty balls in the drum or bubble, and if six have to be correctly selected, what are the odds of those particular numbers coming out? This can be worked out mathematically, but the number is so big that it will not be given here lest it discourage or dishearten potential players, any of whom just might win a lottery. (This will be dealt with more fully in the chapter on probability.) Let us just say Mr X has managed to beat very high odds. He has won a big sum of money with his six numbers, even though the odds against him were very high. He must be very lucky! Because of his win, Mr X becomes an object of local interest and attracts the interest of a reporter who happens to be looking for a 'human interest' story. From her report, we learn that Mr X grew up in a rough neighbourhood (unlucky) in a dysfunctional family (unlucky) where the parents abused alcohol, 'controlled substances' and their three children (unlucky), was sterile due to an attack of mumps in his early years (unlucky, probably), was divorced (could be lucky or unlucky), had little formal education (unlucky) and worked as a badly-paid machine operator in a gloomy factory (unlucky). So, had we met Mr X the day before his lottery win, we would have felt justified in describing him as unlucky. But now, suddenly, he is lucky. His luck has changed. He has proved the truth of Wilson Mizner's statement that the only sure thing about luck was that it would change. Knowing Mr X as we now do, we do not feel quite so jealous or envious. He deserved to win, we say. He was due a break, a change of luck. It gave one a sort of warm glow to see something like this happen. One was inclined to say, 'God is in his heaven, all's right in the world.' So, good luck comes to those who deserve it! This leads us into the world of determinism.

Determinism

This philosophical proposition takes the position that everything that has happened since the beginning of time has been determined by a series of prior events and, consequently, must happen in the way that it happens. If one accepts this, then not only Mr X's win but also his rough neighbourhood, bad parents, mumps, sterility, divorce and uninspiring job were all predetermined from the Big Bang, the moment when many cosmologists believe time and space began. So, everything that happened to Mr X, good and bad, was determined billions of years ago, and there was nothing he or anyone else could have done about it. His whole life had been laid out as the result of countless million causes and effects, stretching back to the beginning of the universe.

There has been much debate as to the exact meaning of determinism and a number of different schools of thought have sprung up. The Incompatibilists hold that determinism leaves no room for free will, while the Compatibilists believe that some free will is permitted. Causal determinists say that all future events are determined by past and present happenings. Perhaps the best known of this school is Pierre-Simon Laplace (1749–1827). In his view, were one to know all the past, the present and the laws of nature, it would be possible to predict the future exactly. There would be perfect predictability, because of determinism.

Newtonian physics portrays a material universe which works in a predictable way. The laws of nature are fixed and, were one to know all about physical matter and the laws by which they operate, it would be possible to predict what would happen in the future. Therefore, if we know the initial condition, all the rest that follows can be predicted. To explain this, the example of a billiard ball is sometimes used. If Ball A, whose position is known, is hit dead-on by Ball B, whose velocity is known, then the point at which Ball A will stop is predictable and can be calculated mathematically.

Going back to our lottery winner, Mr X, not only was his win determined long in advance and brought about by the laws of nature which are unchangeable and are outside his control, but Mr X is also believed by some to be the product of another type of determinism, called environmental determinism. This is the hypothesis that a person's physical environment determines his culture and mindset. He is a product of the area and culture into which he happened to be born and this makes him what he is. Add to that biological determinism – according to which everything he does or thinks was determined by the genes he got from his ancestors – and Mr X does not seem to have had much free room in which to manoeuvre. As if he were not restricted enough already, there is also theological determinism, which propounds that God has already determined long ago what people will do and what will happen to them. This leaves no room for free will. The individual is just doing what they were meant to do. When all this is taken together, there seems to be no way that Mr X could not have won. But was it just random luck that all this was predetermined for Mr X, or was it the result of a long, determined sequence of causes and effects? Maybe it was both, and Mr X was lucky that things were predetermined to work out that way for him.

As we saw earlier, Incompatiblists believe that determinism precludes free will. As with determinism, there is a wide range of views on free will. Some deny any free will, some say we have a limited amount, and others say we were created by God with free will and can do whatever we like and are held accountable for it. So is it a case of 'what will be will be', or do we have free will that we can assert to *prove* we have free will? You decide, as a free agent, to have a cup of tea. Then, to assert further your freedom of will, you change your mind and decide to have coffee instead. Surely, this is a person acting with complete independence. Yes, if you can prove that he was not meant, in the big scheme of things, to have a cup of coffee at this time. Or you pick up the remote control to change the channel on the television. You are an autonomous individual, freely choosing whatever channel you wish from the wide range on offer. Possibly, or maybe this was predetermined billions of years ago at the Big Bang. It is enough to make a person a fatalist and decide that there is no point in doing anything at all and maybe just staying in bed, which may be what you were predetermined to do. We will look at this more closely later.

So it all seems to have been worked out long ago. If you are meant to win the lottery, it will happen no matter what you do or do not do. You do not even have to buy a ticket. If it is your fate, you will get one as a surprise present or pick it up in the street. On the other hand, if you are not destined to win, it does not matter how many tickets you buy, you will not win. It is just your luck.

But maybe you do not need luck to win. Remember Laplace and his assertion that, if one knew all the past and present and the laws of nature, one could predict the future. It is just a simple matter of knowing everything. Let us say that you decide to play the lottery. Because you know everything, you will know all about the initial positions of the balls in the bubble, the mass of each ball, the strength and direction of the force propelling the balls around the bubble, which balls are going to bounce off which balls and where they will end up and what ball they will then hit and with what force and from what angle. You also know the intervals at which the door at the bottom will open and what ball will be over the opening at that instant and drop out. And you will be able to do this for all six balls. You will predict all this, not as some hocus-pocus fortune-teller, but as a super-scientist to whom the future is an open book. Making such a prognosis is no trouble to you because you are The Prognosticator. It is just a matter of knowing everything!

Things are not always as simple as they appear. Some systems appear to become random, or even chaotic, and here our Prognosticator would have a problem. Random or chaotic systems cannot be predicted. He would also run into the Heisenberg Uncertainty Principle, which, put simply, tells us that is not possible to know both the position and velocity of a particle at the same time. We can know one or the other, but not both. This puts a limit on the knowable.

Up to the time of Niels Bohr and the birth of quantum physics, it was generally accepted that things happened in the universe in a completely deterministic way. Quantum mechanics was a severe shock to the system for those who believed in an underlying determinism and found it difficult, or impossible, to accept the quantum physics view that exact positions and momentums do not exist. According to quantum physics, the best we can do is to ascribe probabilities to them. So maybe it is not possible to be the Prognosticator, after all.

Even if you are not in the fortunate position of knowing everything, perhaps there are other ways of going about picking your 'lucky' lottery-winning numbers. You could number little heaps of grain from one to fifty, spread them in a circle on the floor, put a rooster in the centre and note which six heaps it eats first. If that does not sound rational or scientific enough to satisfy you, then you could put fifty numbers in a hat and pick out six, blindfolded. Better yet, why not get a disinterested friend to do it, lest your overpowering desire to win cause your luck to abandon you. Then, there is always the 'gut feeling' which will, no doubt, come up with six numbers that you think will win. You could go online and get 'lucky' numbers or immerse yourself in numerology and then use your knowledge of numbers and their relation to 'reality' to select winners. If you are of a contemplative nature, why not just meditate and then select the first six numbers that come into your head. Finally, if you wish to be relieved of the burden of selecting numbers, then you can get a 'quick pick' at the lottery shop by letting the computer pick your numbers. Then you don your 'lucky' underwear, carry your 'lucky' rabbit's foot, avoid black cats that threaten to cross your path, don't walk under a ladder or break a mirror, and hope for the best. You have done all you can, and now it is a matter of luck. It might all sound very unscientific and random, but then the numbers that come out of the drum are random. There was no scientific way of predicting them, even though it was all cause and effect.

Destiny
Those who believe in destiny accept that events are predestined. They are convinced that the universe has a fixed order, and nothing can be done to alter it. Destiny is similar to fate, but fate is more often used to refer to how things have proceeded up to the present, while destiny looks to the future and how this predicts what is to come. In literature, there are many examples of the futility of trying to fight against destiny. From the Greek tragedies to Thomas Hardy and Hermann Hesse, the protagonist cannot escape his or her destiny, no matter how hard he or she tries. Tess of the d'Urbervilles is just as helpless as Oedipus. It is as if there is something 'out there' that

is going to get them, no matter what. The ancient Romans were a practical people who succeeded in building up a mighty empire, yet they worshipped their goddess Fortuna who turned the wheel of fate blindly, giving rise to chance, uncertainty and, possibly, chaos. The Romans could build up and govern an empire, but accepted that chance, fortune and chaos were always likely to be significant determining factors.

They also had the Parcae, known to the Greeks as the Moirai. These are referred to nowadays as the Fates and were believed to control the lives of men – and some suggested that even the gods were subject to their will. Clotho was the spinner, and on her spindle she spun the thread of life, while Lachesis used her rod to measure the thread of life which each one was to have. The thread was cut by Atropos, who chose the time and manner of a person's death. They were believed to appear when a child was three days old and to lay out its life. The Fates are often portrayed as ugly crones or hags, not unlike the witches in *Macbeth*, but this did not prevent many people from worshipping them as powerful goddesses.

It was not just the Greeks and Romans who believed in such entities. In Norse mythology, the Norns who performed a similar role to the Fates, and other mythologies had similar deities.

The Butterfly Effect

There is no doubt that the weather, at times, can be unpredictable, and even meteorologists using the latest and most sophisticated equipment will not always get the forecast right. Indeed, some scientists suggest that the weather, by its very nature, may be literally unpredictable, which would be the case were it so sensitive as to be affected by something as apparently insignificant as the fluttering of a butterfly's wings. Could the flutter of the wings in the southern hemisphere cause a tornado or tsunami in the northern hemisphere? The slight disturbance caused by the flutter could have a chain-reaction effect which would snowball into a major weather system. No one is suggesting that the butterfly's wing-beat would be the sole cause of a tornado or hurricane, but it could very well be a contributory factor. Small causes can lead to momentous effects.

Suppose a marksman is shooting a bullet at a target. A small move in the position of the rifle muzzle away from the bullseye will result in the bullet being off-target, and the amount by which it is off will be magnified as the distance to the target is increased. The initial condition (slight movement of the muzzle) has resulted in the bullet missing the target.

There have been some fanciful applications of the butterfly effect, particularly with those who like to speculate on time travel and the possible situations to which it could give rise. Take the situation of a man who travels back in time. His presence in the past would no doubt change some immediate event. For example, he might have a micro effect on the weather or his exhalations would increase the amount of carbon dioxide in the atmosphere. This could have unpredictable repercussions in the future and would very likely lead to a different present than would have come to pass had our time traveller not intervened. The reality he had left would not be the one to which he returned and, in that event, he would not have been able to travel back in time. This is a time paradox and is used by some to disprove, or at least to cast serious doubt, on the possibility of time travel. This fanciful scenario is similar in some ways to the situation of the time traveller who goes into the past and kills one of his ancestors, resulting in his never being born.

Could it be that one's good or bad luck is attributable to something as whimsical as the flutter of a butterfly's wings? It would be difficult to prove or disprove. Either way, you could say that it was all determined – meant to happen. The butterfly had to flap its wings and you had to end up where and what you are.

Chapter 3
Magic and Luck

Men of action are favoured by the goddess of luck.
George S Classon

Depend on the rabbit's foot if you will, but remember it didn't work for the rabbit.
R E Shay

Luck never gives; it only lends.
Swedish proverb

Good luck needs no explanation.
Shirley Temple Black

Aboriginal man, and in some cases indigenous and even supposedly sophisticated people in modern times, believed in witchcraft. Witchdoctors, shamans and magicians were believed to have the power to contact spirits and influence the course of things on Earth. This power could be used to help, or abused to harm, the people of the tribe, who generally lived in fear and awe of the practitioners. As societies developed and the nomadic lifestyle gave way to settled agriculture, the witchdoctors adjusted to suit the times. Their job now was to act on behalf of the tribe so that they prospered and evil was kept away. This was done by contacting the gods or spirits, or at least pretending or claiming to do so, and passing on whatever advice or warnings that were received. In time, some of these witchdoctors became shamans or priests, but their role was still very much the same. The will of the gods and spirits had to be known so that man could prosper or, at least, not perish.

Once the wishes of the gods had been ascertained, it was up to the shaman to make sure that they were fulfilled. This often meant sacrifices of agricultural products, animals or even human beings. All this was a small price to pay in return for a secure life. This mode of existence continued until there was good reason to change it. And it was not just in the distant past that it was practised. In Hinduism, there are individuals, known as mantriks, who can use mantras or incantations that are believed to reach into the world of magic. Some believe that ascetics, who have worked for years to discipline their minds and bodies through meditation, privation and other means, may obtain powers that are akin to the supernatural. Some even believe that these ascetics can perform miracles.

In South and Central America, for example, human sacrifices continued down to the time of the conquistadores. Primitive men lived in a harsh world, surrounded by many dangers and a multitude of things which he did not understand and, consequently, feared. While we may regard him, condescendingly, as ignorant or barbaric, he had a good grasp of the practicalities of life. He knew that there was no free lunch. If you wanted to appease the gods, get what you wanted and have good luck, there was a price to pay – rituals had to be followed and sacrifices made. As the gods deserved the best, it was not surprising that man should sacrifice his own kind to them. Nor was it enough to sacrifice to the gods. There were usually an elaborate series of rules which laid down what people should and should not do, and there were people who were to be venerated or shunned. These were called taboos and will be discussed later in the book.

The practice of magic goes back to prehistory and continues up to the present. The Magi of Zoroastrianism and the priests of Egypt passed their lore to the Greek mystery religions. Magic blended into early religion and, for many centuries, it would have been difficult to determine where magic ended and religion began. Indeed, this is still so, as there are New Age practices which blend the two as a unified belief system. Some cynics or atheists might say that some of the most widely accepted religions contain strong elements of ritual, magic and irrational beliefs.

The practice of magic continued through the Dark Ages into the Middle Ages. Here, it acquired a little scientific respectability as learned men, who could read and write or had knowledge beyond that of most people around them, would often be regarded as magicians. This was especially so for the alchemists, who pursued their arcane practices in their quest for the Philosopher's Stone in their attempts to turn base metals into gold. The Catholic Church strongly forbade any practices that smacked of magic or witchcraft, but were unable to eradicate it completely from folk religion. The use of 'magic words', wands or magical tools, magic symbols or the evocation of spirits were strongly condemned but, at the same time, the Church practised the veneration of relics, a practice which some would regard as a type of witchcraft or idolatry.

During the Renaissance, there was an increase in scepticism as to the magical practices and we see the early signs of scientific method. Man began to see more clearly the connection between cause and effect, and he took on a new confidence that the world around him could be understood through reason and logic (as with the Stoics of old). With the Enlightenment and Industrial Revolution, this confidence grew and science was seen as the way to a better future, free from the shackles and fears of magic. This was a time of optimism. Alchemy became chemistry and germs rather than evil spirits were seen as the cause of illness. There was no further need for magic and, surely, its days were numbered.

However, belief in magic has proved remarkably resilient and has evolved, or adapted, to fit new conditions. The thinkers of the Age of Reason regarded themselves as above belief in such hocus-pocus. Britain's Witchcraft Act of 1735 specified that anyone who put themselves forward as being able to call up spirits should be fined, rather than the previous penalties which included being put to death. So, people who claimed to have magical powers were generally regarded as frauds rather than evil. Again, one would think that magic was outdated, but it was not so. During the Romantic period and at the end of the 19th century, interest in magic revived again. Societies such as the Hermetic Order of the Golden Dawn and the Theosophical Society sprang up and began to attract adherents. The 20th century saw an increased interest in magic. Gerald Gardner's *Witchcraft Today* and the writings of Aleister Crowley fuelled that interest. Some who were immersed in the counterculture atmosphere of the 1960s and 1970s proved to be receptive to such ideas. Today, many different types of magic are practised, such as ceremonial magic and Wicca.

The definition of magic may vary from group to group but all are agreed that their purpose is to help the individual, or the planet, and in fact some of their techniques are not so different from those utilised in clinical psychology.

Whatever the brand of magic, or witchcraft, the aim is usually to bring about a change – to control people, events or the laws of nature – by the use of the supernatural. Spells, potions, incantations, magical objects, rituals or the power of the will are used in an effort to achieve those ends. Magicians attempt to prevent effects that they do not desire and to achieve effects which they do. In other words, they are trying to make their own luck and determine the future so as to get what they want and avoid what they do not want. Their aims would not be very different from those who use a rabbit's foot, four-leaf clover, horseshoe or some other 'lucky' object to obtain good fortune. Nor would their aims be very different from a religious person who prays in order to obtain good and avoid evil through the help of God. Their aims would be similar, but their methods different.

In *The Golden Bough* (1890), Sir James George Frazer puts forward the hypothesis that the development of society was from magic to religion to science. To illustrate this, let us take the case of three men with stomach-aches. Early magical man will endeavour to get rid of the pain by magical means. Believing that the amount of pain in the world is fixed, clearly the only way of getting rid of the stomach ache was to pass it on to someone else. How else could it be done, as pain cannot just go nowhere? So, he goes to a crossroads or some frequented pathway, and buries his pain there, believing that the next person who passes will get his pain and he himself will be rid of it. The religious man, in the days when medical science was less well developed than now, but in some cases even today, would look to God for relief from his stomach-ache. A modern, more scientifically-inclined person will go to a doctor and describe the symptoms. The doctor will then try to diagnose the cause of the pain and then treat the cause, thus getting rid of the symptom, the pain. Again, in all cases, the aim is the same – it is just the methods that differ.

There have been a number of theories of magic. Those who participate in magic practices have come up with a number of ideas as to how their craft works but, in general, these have been more concerned with the rituals and objects involved than with questioning how it works. In cases where their magic does not appear to work it generally will not cause doubts as to the efficacy of their practices. Rather, the failure will be ascribed to something that was not done, or done incorrectly. It will be just a matter or doing it again. Some practitioners will claim that magic utilises a force of nature that science has not yet identified, or may never identify. Scientists have identified four fundamental forces of nature – gravity, electromagnetism, and the strong and weak nuclear forces. Some magicians believe that there is a fifth force, one that they can tap into and use to perform their magic. Many people who are involved in paranormal research also believe in the existence of this fifth force, which – they claim – scientists, in their arrogance or ignorance, do not recognise.

Some magicians claim that they are assisted by spirits or beings who have the power to influence the order of nature. Yet others claim the aid of mystical forces, human energy, symbols or the power of the conscious or subconscious mind.

On a more scientific level, Frazer puts forward the hypothesis that belief in the efficacy of magic is the result of faulty thinking. He gives the following definition of sympathetic magic:

> If we analyse the principles of thought on which magic is based they will probably be found to resolve themselves into two; first, that like produces like, or that an effect resembles its cause, and second that things which have once been in contact with each other continue to act on each other at a distance after the physical contact has been severed. The former principle may be called The Law of Similarity, the latter the Law of Contact or Contagion. From the first of these principles, namely the Law of Similarity, the magician infers that he can produce any effect he desires merely by imitating it: from the second he infers that whatever he does to a material object will affect equally the person with whom the object was once in contact, whether it formed part of his body or not.

So, according to the Law of Similarity, the magician who wanted the rain to fall went outside and sprinkled some water into the air and it fell down like raindrops. Of course, this simple procedure was likely to be accompanied by chanting, bodily gyrations or some other ritual or words that would, no doubt, impress those gathered about, who were themselves not fortunate enough to possess such wonderful powers and arcane knowledge. After all this, the rains must surely come.

Belief in the Law of Contact or Contagion caused primitive man to go to great lengths to carefully conceal items such as clipped nails, hair or any other material discarded from the body lest they fall into the hands of a witchdoctor or anyone who was ill-disposed to them. They believed that the possessor of such items would then be in an extremely strong position to work evil on them. A person who did not take precautions in disposing of these substances was playing fast and loose with his luck.

Magicians and shamans in primitive societies were, in their own way, as arrogant as an atheistic modern scientist, whose pride may exceed his knowledge. The magician had no doubt that he could influence the course of nature and men. He believed that he, or indeed she, could cause the crops to fail, dry up the cows, render a man or woman sterile, send a mosquito or snake to bite someone, or cause a person to be struck by lightning. In such a context, it would be very bad luck to get on the wrong side of a magician. It was also inadvisable to make enemies within the village as they might seek the assistance of a magician to bring bad luck to you or a member of your family. If a person was bitten by a mosquito and then developed malaria, this was not seen as just bad luck or the random act of an insect. The question would be asked, 'Who sent the mosquito?' After all, there were any number of other people that the mosquito could have bitten, so why did it choose this particular person? Clearly, the mosquito was acting under the direction of a magician, who had probably been paid by an enemy to direct it at its victim. Similarly with snakebites and lightning. Why had the snake bitten this particular person? Or, of all the people in the village, why was this one particular person hit by lightning? There was no doubt it was the work of a magician or an enemy. These beliefs came from overrating the influence that man had over the natural world and its operations.

But what if the magic did not work? Were it to happen that the magician or witchdoctor went through the required rituals, used the appropriate medicine and carried out all the routine required, but nothing happened – then what? Would he doubt the efficacy of magic and give up his day (or night) job for something more mundane? Hardly likely. Were the magic to fail, then the magician, as stated earlier, would conclude that he had not carried out the ritual correctly and he would give it another try.

Magicians were powerful, feared and respected individuals in primitive societies, and are so even today for those who believe in such practices. However, this power also carried a great responsibility. Basically, the magician had to deliver, to get results. If he were unable to end a drought, keep away the locusts, cause the crops to grow, bring good luck to the village's hunters and fishermen and make sure the sun rose every morning, giving up his day (or night) job might not have been an option. Failure was to be avoided, at least repeated failures for which he could not find a reason or an excuse. It was not unusual for unsuccessful practitioners to be killed or, if they were lucky, driven from the village.

In cases of failure, magicians were usually able to come up with some explanation or excuse that would satisfy the people. They could blame some evil person in the village who was preventing the magic from working and bringing misfortune on the village. This would lead to a witch-hunt for this individual so that he or she could be found and punished. One method of doing this was for the magician to tell the people that there was an evildoer in their midst and that he was going to let the spirits decide who that evil person was. There were a number of ways in which the spirits were believed to be able to do this and often there was nothing very spiritual about it. The magician would usually have decided in advance who was going to be identified as the evil one who was bringing misfortune on the villagers. Then, the witchdoctor prepared a certain poisonous potion that everyone in the village had to drink. The people would then be told that the spirits would single out and kill the evil person or people who were bringing misfortune on the village and preventing the magician from doing his job. As far as the people were concerned, the magician just administered the potion and the rest was up to the spirits. However, to help the spirits in making up their minds, the magician had given a smaller dose of the potion to the person or people whom he wanted to be identified as the malefactors. Before long, the people who had been given the larger doses would become violently sick and start to vomit. Obviously, the spirits were ejecting the poison from their bodies because they were innocent. The person or people who had been given the smaller dose would not vomit, a fact that would soon be noticed by all the others. Their fate was now sealed. Either they would be left for the potion to do its work and kill them or, more likely, they would be set upon by the other villagers and killed for all the misfortune they had brought on them. This was called 'instant justice'. Now the medicine man could do his magic again and, maybe, this time it would work, now that the evil ones were no longer able to exert their malevolent influence.

There is evidence that mankind has practised magic for at least 50,000 years and probably longer. It has been practised in almost all societies around the world. Generally regarded as a highly specialised art, there were, however, occasions on which 'ordinary' people could do a little of it themselves to improve their luck or fend off evil. Magic pervaded every aspect of primitive man's life and this was particularly so in the areas in which luck, as well as skill, played a significant role, such as hunting and fishing. As these activities were vital for the survival of early man, and were daily activities for which a person could not constantly be running to the magician for help, there were certain things that people could do for themselves that would be likely to improve their chances of success. Examples abound in *The Golden Bough*, but the following will give a general idea of what was involved.

Early man had great reverence for animals and fish (whom he often called 'the old ones' as he believed they had always been around) and he was not foolish enough to believe that that fish or game could be taken without the aid of magic. In order to increase his chances of success, a Melanesian fisherman would first make sure that his net was 'magicked'. Fortunately, the process of 'magicking' his net was a relatively simple DIY operation that did not require the expertise of a professional practitioner. The man spread his net on the beach or riverbank. Then he walked away a short distance from the net and stopped. Turning around, he retraced his steps back to the net and accidentally/on purpose got his feet entangled in it. 'What's this?' he cries, all surprised. 'I seem to have become caught in my net.' Now the net is 'magicked' and surely cannot fail to catch fish. Why rely on random luck when you could take measures to improve it?

On the other hand, you could also do things that would be likely to bring on misfortune. A villager who had been offended by something you had said or done, or who was envious of your crops, wife, children, prosperity or good fortune, could go to a witchdoctor and arrange for something unpleasant to happen. If it was the intention to hurt a particular man, it was often the case that the magic was worked on a family member so that the real victim would have to live with the torment and heartache. Killing the offender was generally not regarded as the best solution, as the dead can feel no pain or sorrow.

All this could develop into a vicious circle of fear, suspicion and tit-for-tat retaliation. The man who felt that his wife or child had been injured or killed by the evil of an enemy would naturally want revenge, or justice. Then it was his turn to visit a witchdoctor, identify the suspect and leave matters to the professional. Because of this type of behaviour, people lived for thousands of years in fear and ignorance. When its time came, religion did much to release man from this lamentable condition. With the Biblical 'Eye for an eye and a tooth for a tooth', the matter was dealt with in an equitable, just and transparent fashion that, people hoped, would satisfy all parties and not lead to a vendetta. Things were settled once and for all, and that was the end of it.

The magic of early man and primitive societies is quite different from what is regarded as magic in this modern, scientific age. Surely, one would think, there is no longer much demand for a magician in the global village of today, top-heavy with doctors, psychiatrists, priests, support groups and experts of all types to whom the individual can turn for assistance. Add to that the internet, the mobile phone and all the other wondrous products of modern technology. How could there be any place for magic in all of this? However, as we have seen, magic is remarkably adaptable and resilient, and has managed to retain a place in society. There are still people who claim they can foretell your future and provide you with objects, numbers, spells, rituals or whatever to help you obtain good luck and avoid bad luck. It is the latest version of a practice which could be considered as one of the world's oldest professions, perhaps even older than the one usually credited with that distinction.

However, even all this might not be enough to protect the tribe. Even the best efforts of the witchdoctors might not be able to provide adequate safeguards. It is often thought that primitive societies were chaotic, lawless and disorganised. While there were generally no written laws, or anything resembling a justice department or police force, there were rules to be followed and punishment was handed out for infringements. Primitive they may have been, but they were not chaotic. There were many practices that had to be observed and certain people who were to be venerated or shunned. A long list of do's and don'ts controlled the behaviour of early man. Many of these ancient rules, or laws, are not given much respect when judged by modern standards and are usually referred to, in a somewhat pejorative fashion, as taboos.

Taboos

A taboo generally refers to some action, person, place or words that are considered unlucky, wrong, unacceptable or even dangerous. Of course, some tabooed activities were criminal and were dealt with as such, but many would more correctly be regarded as inadvisable, bad form, rude or uncouth. Taboos cover a wide range of prohibitions. In primitive societies, taboos were pervasive. Early man was surrounded by a whole set of objects, people and places that were considered bad, unlucky or malevolent. In

The Golden Bough, Frazer devotes a lot of attention to taboos and gives an exhaustive list of tabooed people, events and places.

One would be justified in thinking that taboos were created by people to make life safer and to curb some of man's more basic impulses. In *How the Mind Works*, Steven Pinker proposed that taboos are just human instincts and that such beliefs were built into people since time immemorial. Being, to a large extent, unable to engage in what we will call "logical" thinking, and having a somewhat fanciful view of cause and effect, primitive man would have relied heavily on feelings and emotions in developing his relationships with the world around him. Like any other human being, he wanted to obtain good and avoid evil, and taboos were rules that were believed to help him achieve these aims. He was not stupid, but he did not have the knowledge to comprehend his world in a sophisticated way. Not that he would have felt a need to explain why taboos existed, any more than a modern man would feel a need to explain why murder was illegal or urinating in public was antisocial. The taboos were passed down through the generations and followed without question, their origins either not known or not considered relevant.

There were a large number of tabooed persons, objects, places or conditions in early societies and, in some tribal societies, some remain even up to the present. The dead, fishermen, hunters, mourners, widows, widowers, mothers-in-law, kings, chiefs, menstruating women, warriors after a battle and strangers were often tabooed. Such people were considered as unlucky, dangerous or malevolent, and it was generally considered best either to avoid them or to treat them with caution. In some cases – as with the warriors and mourners, both of whom had come in contact with death – there was usually some kind of ritual cleansing or purification before they were permitted to return to the normal society of the village.

With the dead, there was no such simple remedy. Graveyards were avoided, except during funerals or on occasions on which offerings were being made to the dead, as it was a general belief that the dead harboured ill will towards the living, because of envy, jealousy or some desire for revenge. Some societies went to great lengths to prevent the dead from harming them. It was not unusual for mourners to shave their eyebrows or heads to change their appearance in other ways. Often it was prohibited to mention the name of the dead person and some tribes even took the precaution of changing the names of every person in the village so as to make them more difficult to identify. It was not uncommon to move their villages to a new location after a death.

Widows and widowers were considered particularly unlucky, as it was assumed that their dead spouses would be trying to exert their malevolent forces either on or through them. Consequently, no one would want to associate with them. A widower was not welcome on hunting or fishing trips, and some tribes even went as far as expelling them from the village. In going, they were believed to take the bad luck with them, and the rest of the villagers would not have to live in constant fear of misfortune. In many cases, objects which had been used by, or were associated with, the dead person, such as their eating utensils, weapons or tools, were destroyed and discarded, the better to sever any connection with them.

Special precautions were taken with people who had committed suicide. Sometimes the corpse was disfigured before burial as greater deterrence from any attempt to come back in pursuit of its evil purposes. Until relatively modern times, even in communities which considered themselves civilised, such unfortunate people were often buried at a crossroads so that their unhappy, probably vengeful, spirit could not find its way back to its home. Some Christian churches forbade suicides to be buried in sanctified ground.

Kings, chiefs or medicine men were often tabooed because of the powers they were believed to possess. Such power was seen as potentially dangerous to more ordinary mortals. It was often taboo to touch such people, talk to them directly or even look at them. While warrior societies held their heroes in high esteem, there was a certain ambivalence in this admiration. On the one hand, they were heroes, but on the other they were dangerous or unlucky, because of their association with bloodshed and death. Menstruating women were considered unclean and taboo by many societies and were secluded in special huts outside the village until their periods were finished. Strangers were often tabooed and were either prevented from entering a village or some prophylactic measures were taken to prevent them bringing bad luck. Being an unknown quantity, these outsiders might possess some powerful, strange magic. They were treated with suspicion, and it was not considered advisable to take chances with them.

With the rise and spread of religion, man established a different relationship with his deities and spirits and even with his neighbour. Man was asked to love his neighbour and to do good, even to those who hated him. In the major religions, there was no place for hatred, suspicion and revenge. Christianity, Judaism and Islam are strongly opposed to witchcraft or anything that smacks of magic, and steps have frequently been taken throughout history to punish those suspected or proved of being involved in such practices. These religions have no need for those who attempt or claim to be able to reach into the supernatural. They are based on revealed truth, the word of God handed down to the prophets and written down for all humanity. Man can get in touch with God directly, without the use of intermediaries who claim to have such powers. All that man needs to know has been revealed, so there is no need to look further than the sacred texts to find out how to behave and what God expects of him. If anything miraculous is seen to happen, then that is accepted as the work of God and not of some witchdoctor or shaman. God directs the world and the natural order in His infinite wisdom. There is no need for man to attempt to influence or change its course. In the past, harsh treatment was generally meted out by religious officials to those who claimed to have such powers, but nowadays, in our less religious societies, a more relaxed attitude is common, and such people are more often regarded as fakes, quacks or confidence tricksters.

The more recent witch-hunts have generally happened in places where religious or quasi-religious belief was strong, even fanatical, particularly belief in the power of Satan. In the case of the witch-hunts in Salem, Massachusetts, there is evidence that the accusations of witchcraft were not entirely separate from personal jealousies and envy, as has been the case in other places. There were, of course, those who believed that Satan had been called up in their community, and steps had to be taken to rid themselves of this foul presence. For this reason, merely killing the witches was not enough to remove the contagion – they had to be totally destroyed, as far as possible. Such punishments were often carried out in the belief that, while the evil body was destroyed, a witch's immortal soul could be saved.

While taboos are generally associated with primitive tribes, even in modern societies there are a large number of activities that could be described as tabooed. Members of certain religions are forbidden to eat certain foods. Many societies have, or had, tabooed certain types of sexual activity, such as incest, homosexuality, bestiality or necrophilia. On a less serious level, such practices as picking one's nose or breaking wind in public, burping, spitting and public urination are regarded as uncouth and undesirable. While the consumption of alcohol is permitted in most societies, public drunkenness is frowned upon. In the case of 'controlled substances', use is not only forbidden but also illegal. Using obscene language is regarded by many as taboo and discussion of certain topics such as sex, religion and politics is taboo in some cultures. It would therefore be true to say that there are still taboos – though we would be more likely to refer to them as prohibitions or things that are 'just not done'.

Looking back from the vantage point of the early 21st century, there are two broad views regarding taboos. One view is that early man was ignorant, superstitious and primitive. He can hardly be blamed for not knowing better, but we are condescending in our superior way. Others look back at these taboos and try to find good, practical reasons for them. They will say that it was sensible to have mourners purify themselves after a funeral, lest they had contracted some contagion from the dead and might spread it around. One must remember that, as already mentioned, primitive man had no concept of germ theory or microbiology and regarded illness as the work of evil spirits. The purpose of ritual cleansing was to get rid of evil spirits, not germs, though the latter may have been the result. Similarly, a modern psychiatrist or sociologist might say that, in a primitive society, it was a good idea to eject widows and widowers as these now unattached individuals could act as a temptation for others to sexual misbehaviour and were best removed. In their view, it was not fear of the dead that was at work, but fear of social disruption.

We must accept that the mind of primitive man did not work in the same way as that of a modern person. Like any other person, primitive man wanted to have a good life but the way he thought this could be achieved was very different from ours. In this age of relativism, early man does not need any vindication for his beliefs and behaviour. It is only our own beliefs and behaviour that we need to justify. As mentioned earlier, modern society is not totally free from taboos and some of our attitudes towards those who suffer from mental or physical handicaps, or who pursue unconventional sexual lifestyles, might need to be modified. There are those who would claim that many of our class-ridden attitudes are just modern taboos. Each society tries to find its 'comfort zone' and, perhaps, this is the best context in which to look at taboos.

Ordeals

Before our current knowledge of DNA or crime scene evidence, or indeed any well-established techniques of criminal investigation, it was not always easy for people to get justice. In most cases, justice was swift, and sometimes it was rough. We saw earlier how some primitive people identified and punished those whom they believed were guilty of practising malignant magic.

As time went on, methods of proof also changed, especially in western societies that were experiencing the influences of Christianity. In medieval times, once an accusation was made or a person was suspected of having committed a crime, witnesses were called and the evidence examined, as is the practice today. Most cases were disposed of quite rapidly, but there were some in which it was impossible for a jury or judge to decide on the guilt or innocence of an accused. In such an event, they could say, 'Ignoramus' (We do not know). Clearly, such a case was beyond the abilities of man. There was only one way to decide the matter. As always, when man found himself helpless, he turned to a higher power. God would have to decide.

While some of the methods used to get at the truth in cases of witchcraft, murder or robbery might now strike us as quaint or barbaric, we must be careful about judging the past by the standards of today. We must also bear in mind that these ordeals were serious, genuine attempts to find the truth and administer justice. Indeed, the word 'ordeal' comes from an Old English word meaning 'justice' or 'verdict'. Trial by ordeal goes back as far as the Code of Hammurabi (around 1770 BC), when it was used in cases of sorcery. Ordeals were not common in the Dark Ages, but reappeared in the Middle Ages, and were commonly used in the witch trials of the 16th and 17th centuries.

The idea behind ordeals was to make an individual perform some task and then observe the results that ensued. These results were accepted as God giving an answer. In Norman England, ordeals were frequently used to decide cases. However, even here, the social order was respected and upper-class defendants were subjected to ordeal by fire. The hoi polloi usually had to make do with ordeal by water.

Although there were local variations, the ordeal by fire usually required the accused either to walk a distance of nine feet carrying a red-hot iron or to walk on hot iron. The burns were then bandaged, and were examined by a priest three days later. If the hands or feet were not completely healed, the defendant was found guilty and punishment meted out. In serious cases, this was usually either exile or execution. If the burns had healed, then God was believed to have intervened to show the suspect's innocence. One would be inclined to believe that this method yielded quite a high conviction rate as a person would need to have amazing healing powers, or be lucky in some other fashion, in order to be acquitted. The odds were definitely not in the suspect's favour.

The odds were not much better in the ordeal by water. There were two types here, hot and cold. The cold-water ordeal has a long history, going back to the ancient

Babylonians. In essence, the cold-water ordeal involved a suspect being thrown into a river or a barrel of water. If he or she drowned, they were guilty. The belief was that the weight of a person's guilt would draw them down. Those who survived were declared innocent. Lucky the man or woman who could swim or tread water, or was positively buoyant! In Tudor and Stuart times, a variation of this method was used which decidedly reduced the odds of an innocent verdict. Effectively, Cold Water Ordeal Version 2 reduced to zero the odds of a fortuitous outcome for the unfortunate suspect. If the accused sank, and presumably drowned, then he or she was declared innocent. Floating was also proof of guilt. It is difficult to see the hand of God in Version 2, but that did not mean that contemporary apologists did not try to justify it. One hypothesis was that witches were exceptionally light, though no explanation was given as to why this might be. One also doubts that a weighing scale was used to measure the lightness. Even if the witches were rather light, this was more likely to be the result of the privations of incarceration – be they starvation or illness – than the work of Satan.

Ordeal by hot water was similar to the ordeal by hot iron, only hot water replaced hot metal. The accused had to put his or her hand into a pot of boiling water. The hand was then bandaged and checked after three days. Guilt or innocence was determined by the condition of the burned flesh.

Bearing all this in mind, we must consider ourselves lucky to live in more enlightened times. In most countries, at least, a person gets a 'fair trial' or at least 'due process', though the quality of justice may be influenced by how much money a person can afford to spend on their defence. Yes, we are lucky to live in times when hot or cold water or hot metal are not used to determine guilt or innocence. Such practices went out in the 16th century. But the reason they were no longer used was that they were replaced by a procedure which was thought to be more effective at getting at the truth – torture. Whipping and other forms of 'persuasion' were used in ancient times to get information from people, but systematic torture was not generally used as a matter of policy. It is known that a method known as 'pressing' was used in early Tudor times. A rock was placed under a person's back and then weight was put on their chest. Unless the person talked, the procedure usually proved fatal in a few days as the weight was gradually increased. As a means of getting at the truth, or at least of getting people to 'talk', torture has proved to be popular. It has stood the test of time, and is still used in many parts of the world. To make it more effective, we now have the modern tools of electricity, drugs and technology that were not available in earlier times. Indeed, we are lucky.

Chapter 4
Philosophy, Religion and Luck

All of us have bad luck and good luck. The man who persists through the bad luck – who keeps right on going – is the man who is there when the good luck comes – and is ready to receive it.
Robert Collier

Don't believe in miracles – depend on them.
Laurence J Peter

For the truly faithful, no miracle is necessary. For those who doubt, no miracle is sufficient.
Nancy Gibbs

This book is not meant to be a treatise on philosophy or comparative religions, but since both have been, and continue to be, a huge influence in the lives of billions of people, it might be of interest to see what they have to say, if anything, on the subject of luck and the degree of control a person has over his or her life.

While most of the classical philosophers allowed that chance, or luck, played a part in the lives of mortals – that much was in 'the lap of the gods' – they nevertheless made strenuous efforts to use reason and logic to find a natural, and hopefully pleasant, path through life. These were serious attempts to understand the world around them. Although religions may not use the word 'luck', referring instead to 'the will of God' or 'the grace of God', if it is seen that all things come from God, then surely destiny, fate or luck are within His domain. If God is seen as omnipotent, then He has the power to cause anything to happen or prevent anything from happening. Some of the good or evil that comes a person's way during life may be regarded as deserved, but in cases where events were outside their control, it seems justifiable for a religious person to speak of luck or 'the will of God'.

Philosophy

Before we look at religions and their approaches to luck, we will take a brief glance at classical philosophy and try to determine its world view. For hundreds of years before Christianity, philosophers (meaning 'lovers of wisdom'), particularly in Greece, had been contemplating the human condition and trying to determine such things as truth and how a person should proceed through life. The philosophers endeavoured to understand the world in which they found themselves and attempted to find a route through life that was rational and satisfied their understanding of man and the universe. While not exactly religions, as they did not base their beliefs on revealed truth – nor were God or gods given the same prominence as in religion – they were sincere and intelligent attempts to gain knowledge and wisdom. Some of the ideas of these Ancient Greek philosophers, such as Aristotle and Plato, found their way into Christian ethics.

One philosophy which had a strong influence on early Christian thought, and which in a way bridged the worlds of philosophy and religion, was Stoicism. It was founded by Zeno in the 3rd century BC, and called Stoicism after the porch (*stoa*) near the Agora in Athens where Zeno taught his classes in full public view. While believing that the universe was deterministic, the Stoics tried to learn how this affected the freedom of man. They believed that in order to comprehend universal wisdom, man had to suppress emotions that would cloud rational judgement. The Stoics also taught that a person was judged not by their words but by their actions, similar to the Biblical 'by their deeds ye shall know them'. They believed in virtue and the virtuous man was seen as one who lived in accord with nature. One had no control over the universe but one could achieve harmony and happiness by virtue and the use of logical, rational thinking. The universe they regarded as God or nature and all things were subject to Fate. The universe was one collective soul, man being only one small part of it. His best path through life was to follow Reason and blend in with nature.

It would be incorrect to understand the ancient Stoics in the modern sense of the word 'stoical' as being 'long-suffering'. 'Stoical calm' was achieved, according to Zeno, not by ignoring or not caring about things, but by using Reason to achieve understanding, knowledge and wisdom. Justice, wisdom, courage and temperance were regarded as the most important qualities in life. Logic, dialogue, mental discipline and avoidance of ignorance or falsity caused by irrational emotions were the means of obtaining these qualities.

According to the Stoics, all men were part of one big, universal spirit. Not much importance was given to a person's financial standing or social position and, in an age when slavery was generally accepted without question, the Stoics taught that all human beings were naturally equal. Although the Stoics did not speak of luck, they believed in Fate and the man who had achieved some knowledge and wisdom would be expected not only to accept his Fate but also to accept responsibility for whatever parts of his life were within his control. Man was not in control of his destiny but he was in control of how he responded to what happened to him.

Although the Church fathers regarded Stoicism as pagan, many Stoic concepts were incorporated into Christianity. Both regarded man as weak or evil, both felt that the passions had to be controlled and that the individual could improve himself. However, what was regarded as Stoic pantheism did not fit in with the Christian concept of God, and Stoics did not refer to reward or punishment after death.

Stoicism gained wide popularity, not just in Greece but throughout the Roman Empire. It attracted such famous Greeks as Epictetus, but probably its most famous disciple was the Roman emperor Marcus Aurelius. Even after all these years, reading his *Meditations* one is struck by his wisdom, compassion and desire to be virtuous. However, another Roman emperor, not very long after Marcus Aurelius, took a very different view. In 529 AD, Emperor Justinian I closed the schools of philosophy as he regarded their 'pagan' beliefs as not being in keeping with the burgeoning Roman Catholic Church. Though philosophy was no longer held in the same regard, its influence was not lost forever. Its regard for logic and reason, the belief that man could understand his world and did not have to live in abject fear of his gods in a universe which he believed to be incomprehensible, became dormant for a number of centuries. The Renaissance saw a rebirth of interest in philosophy and the classical world. The spirit of questioning began to replace that of acceptance and faith. This led to the Age of Reason in which man took on a new confidence that he could not only understand his world, but also shape and direct it. One would think that this would put an end to belief in luck, providence and fate, but this did not happen. The sciences developed and expanded the fields of human knowledge. Determinism came to be accepted as a force of nature, and chance again came to be seen as a significant force in people's lives, albeit as the outcome of cause and effect.

Religion

It is not known exactly when mankind first conceived the idea of a God or gods, or started to make sacrifices to a being or beings that they regarded as being superior to, and having power over, them. Archaeologists have found evidence at very early burial sites that ancient man buried his dead with a certain amount of ritual that would seem to indicate a belief in a continuation of some form of life in a domain beyond the grave or, perhaps, a fear of the spirits of the dead. Either way, it shows that man had begun to think that there might be some part of him that continued to exist after death. Early societies were polytheistic and there was usually a multiplicity of gods for various aspects of life and nature.

Early man's relationship with his gods was often very direct and sometimes very pragmatic. It was often the case that people in a particular area worshipped particular gods, tried to ensure that they did not displease them and made offerings to appease them. Often images of these gods were set up in public places or in sites which were considered sacred, but later 'household' gods would be kept by each family. If the people moved, or were forced out of their area, and settled elsewhere, they often abandoned their old gods and took up the worship of the gods that were worshipped in their new location. This was particularly so if the people had been forced out, as there would be resentment with the gods who had been seen as not assisting them or being less powerful than the gods of the invaders. Changing allegiance was a practical measure as, if they wished to prosper in their new home, they were more likely to do so by worshipping the resident gods, rather than remaining loyal to their own who, whether or not they had failed them, were unlikely to have influence in their new abode.

When the Israelites returned to the Promised Land from their exile in Egypt, they defeated all those who stood in their way. Worshipping the God Yahweh, they seemed invincible under the leadership of Joshua, and their outstanding success was generally regarded as proof that Yahweh was the True God. Those who worshipped other gods, and were suffering defeats, could not but be impressed by the Israelite victories and the God in whose name they were victorious. In such a situation, it would not be surprising if the defeated had serious doubts about the efficacy of their own gods and felt either that they had been abandoned by their gods or had somehow offended them and were now suffering the punishment. Clearly, their gods must be inferior to that of the conquerors.

We now start to see the beginnings of monotheism – the belief that there was one Superior Being who had power over all creation. There was no longer any need for a large number of departmental gods who held sway over discrete areas. Monotheism did not gain rapid general acceptance and we know that the Greeks, Romans, Celts, Vikings and others believed in manifold gods. Many societies that held such beliefs continued to do so long after the time of Jesus and the beginning of Christianity. Indeed, it continues today. Hindus believe in a large number of gods, but most of the other great religions, such as Islam, Christianity and Judaism, are strictly monotheistic.

Early man believed that the gods, or spirits, had great power over his life, for good or evil. In order to get blessings from them and not give offence, offerings and sacrifices were made, ranging from plants to animals and even human beings. When man began to abandon polytheism in favour of monotheism, the break was not sudden and, in many cases, was painful. It would have been difficult at times to say where the dividing line between magic and religion lay, as many people who professed Christian beliefs were reluctant, and perhaps apprehensive, about abandoning their old gods and practices. There was always the danger that one could, unknowingly, offend and then suffer misfortune. It was often difficult for ancient man to establish equilibrium in his relationship with God or the gods. But, in some ways, it was easier for him than for people today. He believed in higher beings that controlled his life and thus felt he knew where good or ill came from – whereas modern man, sceptical or agnostic, is not even sure that there is a God and, if there is, how he should approach Him to obtain the good things in life and reward in the hereafter. The words 'God moves in mysterious ways' show that man is not in a position to understand God or his ways, and humans are left wrestling with inexplicable things which a religious adviser would tell them were 'the Will of God' or a 'mystery of Faith'.

As the Bible contains books going back into the reaches of antiquity and the dawn of monotheism, it is of interest to see what it has to say, if anything, about luck. The word 'luck', or at least any word that has been translated as such, is not found in any English-language edition. However, words that could be construed as 'fate' or 'destiny' do occur. When the Bible tells us that 'evil befell' someone, it sounds very much as if they had experienced bad luck. However, if luck is taken as meaning 'chance', and that things could happen 'by chance', this is not in tune with the general tone of the Bible. Einstein said that God did not play dice and the Bible generally portrays events as being the 'Will of God'. But it is known that the ancient Semites had gods of fortune and fate known as 'Gad' and 'Meni', although they make only cameo appearances in the Bible.

Luck in the Bible

Of the references in the Bible to 'chance' and 'fate' that could be interpreted as luck, or more exactly as the Will of God, the most famous is Ecclesiastes 9:11–12:

> I have seen something else under the sun. The race is not to the swift or the battle to the strong, nor does food come to the wise or wealth to the brilliant or favour to the learned; but time and chance happens to them all. / Moreover, no man knows when his hour will come.

Another quotation often used in relation to chance is Proverbs 16:33, 'The lot is cast into the lap. But every action is from the Lord.'

Casting the lot was used in biblical times to decide on cases which people were unable to resolve. These were often serious, involving life and death. From Proverbs we can see that casting the lot was a way of allowing God to show His will through a random human act. Casting the lot could also be used in the manner of a gamble, as with the Roman soldiers casting lots for the cloak of Jesus after the Crucifixion.

From the Bible, we also learn that God is omniscient. He has all knowledge of the past, present and future, of all that was, is and will be. Following from this, God must know all that will happen in the universe in the future, including what is to happen in the lives of those who live on planet Earth. Then, if God knows everything that is going to happen, maybe it is all laid out in His mind. There are those who take it one step further and state that not only does God know what is going to happen, but He also determined everything that was going to happen, including the destinies of his final creation, man. This echoes scientific determinism, which we discussed earlier.

In some religions, the belief that God had planned all that would ever happen in the universe gave rise to the belief that man had no free will. How could he have free will if God had already determined everything he would or would not do? This later gave rise to the belief known as predestination – that a person's whole life, and even whether they would go to Heaven or Hell, was predestined, and there was nothing a person could do about it. However, this belief did not become widespread until the time of Calvin, just after Luther had started the Reformation in the 16th century. The early Church fathers did not believe in predestination. They accepted that man was sinful and wicked, because of the original sin of Adam and Eve. He was a fallen creature, but God's love had redeemed him and, in the sacrament of baptism, original sin was wiped away and he was given a clean slate. In their view, man had freedom of choice as he had been given free will and could choose his path through life, deciding whether to be good or evil, and reaping the reward or punishment that would follow on Judgement Day. It was not a matter of God having decided one's fate or destiny in advance – one made one's own destiny. But before very long, the Church fathers found themselves having to defend this position against the Cynics and Gnostics and Manichean teachings. Manichaeism – seen by the Christian Church as heretical – held that, because man was born with flaws, he could not make valid free will choices and was, therefore, not responsible for the evil he did. Such a position was anathema to the Roman Catholic Church, which taught that man was responsible for his deeds and that, with prayer and the assistance of a loving God, he would choose the good, avoid evil and thus gain eternal life in Paradise.

This was the prevailing, orthodox view up until the 5th century, when Augustine of Hippo began to question it. Augustine doubted the existence of free will and said that if man was to be saved he needed God's grace. Without this grace, granted by God, man could not be saved. Many in the church saw Augustine as going against the teachings of the Apostle Paul and it was not long before he ran into strong opposition. Bishop Julian of Eclanum accused him of trying to bring back Manichaeism. The supposedly British monk Pelagius was another notable opponent of Augustine and held that man could achieve salvation by the use of his free will. Augustine won out at the Council of Ephesus in 431 and Pelagianism was condemned. A large number of Christians did not accept Augustine's views and the general belief was that man was a free agent and not some kind of puppet or automaton that was following a preprogrammed path.

Lutheranism

For about 1,000 years after this, the Catholic Church went unchallenged without any major heresies or schisms – or at least any that gained broad acceptance. This changed in 1517 when a German monk Martin Luther posted 95 theses on the door of the church in Wittenberg. The theses were an invitation to discuss various aspects of Church doctrine with which Luther was not happy. The monolithic Roman Catholic Church found itself faced with the most serious challenge to its authority in its long history. There had been heresies and schisms, but nothing as serious as that posed by Luther. Inviting the public to discuss these 95 theses would seem to be a fair and democratic ways of getting at the truth, but this was not how things worked in the early 16th century. Luther was seen as a troublemaker and was outlawed, meaning that he could be killed on sight by anyone who was so minded. However, as with many things in life, the theses became political, and a number of German princes quickly saw them as a way of opposing the power of Emperor Charles V and increasing their own autonomy. As it happened, the theses were ideas whose time had come, and they were not just going to disappear.

The main point on which Luther disagreed with the Roman Catholic Church was on the issue of 'justification' by grace through Faith alone because of Christ. The Roman Church stressed 'faith and works'. Luther encouraged people to read the Bible and let it, alone, be their guide. According to him, there was no need for a Pope, priests or any hierarchy to interpret it. He held that only the grace of God could save a person, and that this grace was attained through Faith alone. God had created the world perfect, but Adam and Eve had disobeyed God, and thus brought sin into the world, a sin that was passed down to every human being as original sin. Because of original sin, all human beings should be damned forever, but a loving God does not want anyone to go to Hell for eternity. So, only the grace of God can save sinful man. Luther taught that God gives this grace to certain people who have Faith. However, not all who have this Faith – which in itself is also God's gift – will be saved. Faith does not earn or cause salvation, but salvation flows through Faith. It was all very much in the hands of God, and there did not appear to be much a person could do about it. It was a matter of one's fate, destiny or luck. Salvation was an act of God alone, so fallen man, the children of Adam and Eve, had no power, free will or choice in the matter. Luther also taught that those who are chosen – the 'elect' – are predestined to be saved. Christians who have Faith in Christ are assured of salvation but, again, this Faith is a gift of God, given or withheld as He decides. People, however, are not predestined to an eternity in Hell. Hell is the punishment for sin, for not believing and for lacking Faith.

This is only a small part of the body of doctrine which goes to make up Lutheranism. To complicate matters further, there are many Lutheran churches holding different beliefs on various aspects of doctrine. We have been more concerned here with early Lutheranism and its beliefs relating to God, man and free will, and how much control man had over his life, both here and in determining his place in the hereafter. Luther left very little room for free will. He compared the will to a saddled horse, over the right to mount which God and the Devil fought. The destiny of the individual is decided by who happens to win each individual contest.

Calvinism

Calvinism, also referred to as reformed theology, reformed faith or reformed tradition, was founded by John Calvin, a Frenchman. The two central tenets of Calvinism, at least at its inception, were predestination and the complete depravity of man. Man is a fallen creature who, because of original sin, is incapable of following God. Intervention by God is all that can help him, and only God's mercy can save him. This mercy is given to some but not to others. Were God to condemn all mankind, Calvin taught, it would be no more than he deserved, but, because of His love for man, He decides to save some. A person is not saved because of virtue or Faith but because God shows mercy to them. Belief in the gospel is necessary for salvation, and so is Faith, but these are God's gifts and a sign of His mercy.

Calvin also taught conditional election, which is the doctrine that God chose people to be saved from the beginning of eternity, not because He already knew who would have Faith and live righteous lives, but only because of His mercy. While the

Roman Catholic Church teaches that Jesus atoned for the sins of all mankind by dying on the cross, Calvin taught limited atonement, saying that Jesus atoned only for the sins of those He had chosen for eternal reward. Those whose sins were not atoned for would not be among the elect.

As with Lutheranism, there are many different shades of belief related to Calvinism and it would take us away from our main theme were we to attempt to deal with them in detail. What is of interest to us is whether luck can be seen as the will of God and how various religions interpret it. If, as we have seen with Calvinism, and, perhaps, to a lesser extent, Lutheranism, everything is in the hands of God, then everything is out of the control of man and the individual can do nothing to obtain God's grace, blessings or salvation. In that event, one might call what God decides for a person their 'fate' or 'destiny' and, lucky or unlucky, they have to accept it. If we want to put it in a religious or theological context, then fate, destiny, chance and luck are the will of God and, therefore, not comprehensible by man's finite mind. Those who had been given the grace of God, or had been chosen as the elect, could equally be described as lucky or blessed. It was not for sinful man to enquire as to why some were chosen and others not, for how can the finite comprehend the infinite?

While all Christian reformers look to the Bible for support, even proof, of what they are propounding, it was sometimes a matter of where one looked in the Bible, and how what they read there was interpreted. While one may find passages that appear to support predestination, there are also texts which can be interpreted as showing that humankind has free will:

> If you abide with Me, and my words abide in you, you will ask what you desire and it will be done for you. (John 15:7)

> He who believes and is baptised will be saved; but he who does not believe will be condemned. (Mark 16:16)
> If you confess with your mouths the Lord Jesus and believe in your heart that God has raised Him from the dead, you will be saved. (Romans 10:9)

Much was left to the individual, as the Protestant reformers encouraged the faithful to read the Bible so they could find things out for themselves, something which the Roman Catholic Church had not done. Luther, Calvin, Zwingli and the other reformers of the 16th century were the product of the Renaissance, which had opened up a new spirit of enquiry and brought an end to what has become known as the Dark Ages. Each reformer believed that he had reached into the heart of truth, which was there in the Bible for all to see. For those who accepted the new religious ideas, the relationship with God was changed – but Christian unity was shattered.

Judaism

Reform Judaism does not accept predestination. Many scholars believe that, in the biblical era, Judaism did not teach that God was omniscient or omnipotent, and that this was a later development. Again, the difficulty is translation, as there can be different interpretations of these words. This had an important bearing on whether or not man was believed to have free will. The Spanish Jewish philosopher Hasdai Crescas (c.1340–c.1410) declared that free will did not exist but this was because the universe is deterministic, not because God predicted or laid out people's destinies. However, most followers of Judaism do not follow this view. The vast majority of Jews, whether Reform, Orthodox, Conservative or secular, and whether or not they believe in the omniscience of God, believe that man has free will. As in other religions, attempts have been made to reconcile the two views that man has free will but God knows in advance what people will do.

Islam

The Arabic phrase *al-qaba wa al qadar* is usually translated as 'the Divine decree and the predestination' and lies at the heart of the Islamic view of free will. Muslims accept that Allah (God) is omnipotent, but man still has free will. Just because Allah knows what a person will do, does not take away the person's free will and freedom of choice.

There is, however, the difficulty that since God is omnipotent, He can cause anything to happen or prevent anything from happening. So, it is argued, if Allah allowed something to happen, or did not prevent it from happening, then that was His will. This, in itself, does not take away a person's control over his or her life, but it does mean that whatever happens is the Will of Allah. Often a Muslim will end a sentence with the phrase *Inshallah*, which means, 'If it is the Will of Allah'. This is often used in simple, everyday, situations such as 'I'll meet you tomorrow at noon, *inshallah'*. This is saying that the person will meet you at noon if Allah wills that he is to do so. Perhaps something unexpected will occur that might prevent him meeting you, and it is in acknowledgement of this uncertainty and man's lack of control over his future and what may come to pass that he says *inshallah*. As well as accepting that what is to happen is the will of Allah, Muslims also show their acceptance of whatever happens by saying *mashallah*, which can be translated as 'thank Allah'. This word is used even on occasions on which events have occurred that, on the face of it, are tragic or unfortunate, such as a death or serious illness. It is recognition that man does not know the will or purposes of Allah and must therefore accept what happens, without question. Shia Islam tends to hold more strongly the belief that man has free will and has more control over his destiny.

There is no doubt that some people of various faiths can tend to take to extremes the view that everything that happens is the will of a supreme being and, thereby, shrug off all responsibility for their lives. This is generally not the spirit in which the message of the sacred texts is meant to be understood, but a strict literal and selective reading of them could be used to justify it. The general view of the main religions is that, while God is omnipotent and omniscient, mankind still has a large measure of freedom and choice, and must accept at least some of the blame for evil or misfortune that befalls him. The texts do not encourage humankind to opt out and throw up their collective hands in helplessness, but rather to do their best and leave the rest to God.

The story is told that the Prophet Mohammed was standing outside his mosque in Medina one evening just as the muezzin was ending the call to prayer. A man came along riding a camel. He stopped, dismounted, and was making his way towards the mosque when the Prophet advised him to tie up his camel. The man replied that there was no need to tie up his camel. 'Allah will take care of my camel,' he said. 'Yes, Allah will take care of your camel,' the Prophet replied, 'but first tie it up.'

Indeed, far from absolving man from blame for his actions, Islam is more stringent that some other beliefs in apportioning blame and responsibility to those that others might regard as innocent. For example, if a car is parked on the side of the street and another car crashes into it, then the owner of the parked car is held partially responsible for what has happened, and will be expected to pay a portion of the costs. The thinking here is that, if the parked car had not been there, the other driver would not have hit it. Of course, the driver who hit the parked car will bear the brunt of the blame and expenses, but the owners of both vehicles are seen as being a contributory factor in the accident. What happened was the Will of Allah and everyone will be expected to accept it with a *mashallah*.

Hinduism

Predestination is not a major part of any of the four main schools of Hinduism. Hindus believe in karma, which does not deny free will. *Karma* means 'deed' or 'action', and is seen as operating according to the cycle of causes and effects known as *samsara*. One is responsible for one's own life, as the law of karma says past, present and future are the result of all deeds. People, and in some views even other life forms, are responsible for their karma, which are their actions and the result of their actions. It is like the natural law of cause and effect, action and reaction. People make their choices and reap what they sow. Karma also includes actions and their results from previous lives, all determining a person's future. This is known as accumulated karma. It would be wrong to see karma as retribution – rather it is just the results, or consequences, of previous actions. As the spirit or being is believed to pass from one body to another, it seems only fair that this accumulated karma should be accepted as earned and taken as such. Karma is often seen as 'what goes around, comes around', but one has to take the long view here and would need to know about the spirit's previous incarnations before one could say whether what happens to an individual in one incarnation is fair or unfair, lucky or unlucky.

Reincarnation

Reincarnation means 'to be made flesh again', and is the belief that, when a person dies, they are reborn. Some adherents believe that the soul is reborn in a human being but others say that the soul may also return as an animal or plant. Just how much of the person's soul or 'self' is reborn in the new body is the subject of much disagreement. The law of karma works through the various reincarnations, the belief being that the living of a good life causes the soul to be reborn into a higher, more refined state, while a badly-spent life demotes the soul to a lower form of existence. To those who accept the idea of reincarnation, the present 'self' is the product of all the previous lives the soul has experienced. The soul has to go on being reborn until it reaches the state known to Hindus as *moksha*.

Karma, meaning action, is the law that operates the cycle. In the context of a person's life, it is the accumulated total of all their past lives, and has determined one's present state, as well as future reincarnations. Some people have linked this to determinism, lack of free will and luck. If an individual is the product of previous lives, then, in this life, he has no choice in what he is, or does, because it has all been determined by the previous lives. It is the same with future incarnations, as they will be determined by past lives and the present life. So, if a person has what is called 'good luck', then that person has accumulated a kind of karmic credit over a series of lives that has caused his present good fortune. He or she might be what Henry Ford called 'an old soul' in an article in the *San Francisco Examiner* of 20 August 1928. Ford, a believer in reincarnation, said: 'Genius is experience. Some seem to think that it is a gift or talent, but it is the fruit of long experience in many lives. Some are older souls than others, and so they know more.' Could it be that luck, like genius, is the gift of 'old souls'? Some might disagree with this and say that 'old souls', the products of many previous virtuous lives, would have more refined spirits and would therefore be more concerned with aesthetic or eternal matters. However, if the 'old souls' know more, then it would not be surprising if they were to come up with new ideas or inventions, make wise decisions, become successful and thereby appear lucky.

Whether or not reincarnation can account for luck, there is a wide body of belief, stretching from the distant past right up to the present, that the soul or 'self' goes through a series of lives in accordance with the law of karma. Old bodies are shed, as a snake sheds its old skin, but the soul continues on its path to its destiny. The earliest known references to reincarnation go back to the Hindu scripture *Bhagavad Gita* (at least 2nd century BC), while karma is mentioned in the Upanishads (perhaps from the 6th century BC). Belief in various forms of reincarnation is found in Jainism, Sikhism, Taoism, Buddhism, Christianity and Gnosticism. It is found among Native Americans and the Inuit, and in Norse mythology. The writings of Giordano Bruno (16th century), W B Yeats, Herman Hesse, Edgar Cayce and Henry Ford make references to it. Belief in some form of reincarnation is found in theosophy, anthroposophy, Scientology and New Age beliefs. While many of these groups and individuals believe in quite different forms of reincarnation, the central idea – that man is reborn – is the thread that runs through all of them.

While Orthodox Christianity and Islam would not subscribe to a belief in reincarnation – believing instead that man dies but is raised from the dead by God and is rewarded or punished according to the life he has lived – there are sects or schools within these religions that hold, or held, beliefs in reincarnation. The Liberal Catholic Church, the Christian Spiritualist Movement, the Christian Community and the Unity Church, among others, hold beliefs in reincarnation. Sunni and Shia Muslims do not accept reincarnation but most Ismailis believe in it, and claim to be able to prove it by reference to the Koran. Those who disagree claim that it is based on an erroneous interpretation of the verses.

Orthodox Judaism does not contain belief in reincarnation but, from the late Middle Ages onwards, there are folk beliefs that accepted the idea of rebirth and successive lives.

There has been some scientific study of reincarnation. Professor Ian Stevenson of the University of Virginia wrote extensively on the subject. He produced examples of individuals who were able to give details of people, places and events from the past, of which they could not reasonably be expected to have had knowledge. Could this be people remembering past lives? Stevenson was convinced of the efficacy and exactness of his methods and presented many well-documented statements to support his claims. He is not the only scientist who has accepted reincarnation as a real phenomenon, but the broad scientific community does not accept that anything that has been produced on the matter amounts to proof, and holds that more research is needed before the issue can be resolved one way or the other. The difficulty is that there is no known explanation of how a person could overcome death and then have his spirit transferred into another body.

We have seen that there is a wide range of religious views about whether or not man has free will and just how much control he has over his life. If someone believes that free will does not exist, that life is deterministic, and that no one has any influence over what happens to them, it would hardly be surprising were they to believe in luck, fate or destiny. Is it just a matter of chance, a decision by a creator we have no way of understanding, whether one is rich or poor, healthy or unhealthy, successful or unsuccessful? If it is all predetermined – just cause and effect playing itself out since the Big Bang – then it is surely just the luck of the draw.

Divine Providence

Divine Providence relates to God's power over his creation. The word 'providence' is derived from the Latin *providentia*, usually translated as 'foresight' or 'forethought'. It formed a significant part of the theology of John Calvin, in which God was seen as having complete sovereignty over the world. Calvin taught that it followed from this that man had no free will, as God predestined everything. Were man to think he could somehow understand, let alone control, Divine Providence, it would just be further proof of his innate evil and his failure to understand the will of God. Divine Providence was closely connected to predestination.

Martin Luther took the view that Divine Providence was God creating the world and giving sinful man everything that was required for his well-being. Before Luther, Saint Thomas Aquinas, in his *Summa Theologica*, defined Divine Providence as God's looking after the universe. Man should believe in the goodness of God, who was guiding the universe with a loving hand.

In Jewish theology, there were a number of views on Divine Providence, of which two have gained wider acceptance. One view holds that Divine Providence can sometimes extend to God intervening in the natural order to cause miracles. The second school of thought teaches that miracles are possible in the natural order. As always, there is the difficulty of finite man trying to comprehend an infinite God. Some regard such attempts as presumptive arrogance, and just further proof of man's sinfulness. After all, it was the disobedience of Adam and Eve that caused man to be born into sinfulness, a fallen creature who deserved eternal damnation rather than Divine Providence.

Others, however, take the view that man is justified in attempting to comprehend God's plan through meditation, prayer or study of the natural world, so long as this is done in a spirit of humility and a genuine love of truth. Such people will point to the Bible that tells us God created man in His own image and likeness and, therefore, that the operation of God's will should not be totally outside man's understanding.

Chapter 5
Probability and Luck

Many an opportunity is lost because a man is out looking for four-leaf clovers.
Anon

Luck is not something you can mention in the presence of self-made men.
E B White

Life is what happens to you while you are busy making other plans.
John Lennon

The best laid plans of mice and men do oft-times gang awry.
Robert Burns

It may be that the race is not always to the swift nor the battle to the strong – but that is the way to bet.
Damon Runyon

Probability can be defined as the likelihood that something (an event) will or will not happen. In other words, it is the likelihood of a certain outcome, or how probable or improbable an event is. Not much scientific study was done on probability until the days of Fermat and Huygens in the mid-17th century. Since that time, there have been significant advances in the study of probability, but many would hold it has not reached the level of an exact science. If the number of possible outcomes is very large, and there is randomness involved, then it becomes difficult or impossible to determine probabilities.

Despite this, insurance companies, government departments and others have a vested interest in trying to determine the probability of certain events. An actuary employed by an insurance company has to determine the risk, and potential cost, involved in certain situations. In this modern, computerised age not every individual insurance policy has to be separately calculated. Take the case of a 20-year-old male driver who wants to insure a car. The insurance company will have statistics on the percentage of accidents in which male drivers between the ages of, say, 18 and 25, are involved. This information will be factored into the cost of the insurance policy. Another consideration will be the type of car being insured. If the car is a high-powered sports model, then the cost of the premium will be higher than if it were a one-litre saloon. Other factors will also be taken into account. Does the driver have a full or provisional driving licence? Has he ever had an accident or been convicted of a motoring offence? How many miles does he normally drive in a year, and is this mainly urban or rural driving? Does he require comprehensive or only third party cover? Does he suffer from any physical or mental condition that might affect his driving? All these and more will be factors in deciding the cost of the premium. The insurance company wants to know as much as possible about the driver and his vehicle to determine, as accurately as possible, the risks involved, and will adjust the policy accordingly. The greater the anticipated possibility of a claim, the higher the risk and the higher the premium. For a female driver of 20 the cost will not be the same, as the accident statistics for female drivers between 18 and 25 will be different from those for male drivers. A healthy, middle-aged, man or woman with a good driving record can expect a reduced premium and a better no-claims discount, as they are considered less likely to have an accident and make a claim against their insurance. An older driver, who is more likely to suffer from some visual, aural or other impairment, can expect to have his or her policy adjusted accordingly.

In coming up with a five-year plan, governments will want to know as much as possible of the probability of certain events in the future, such as population growth, so that provision can be made for them. Often present trends can be applied to the future, but there is always the unexpected. Traders on the commodity markets will also be concerned with probability. A trader dealing in coffee beans will want to know the probability of a good or bad harvest, as this will affect the price of beans. Similarly, those involved in the oil market will have a keen interest in anything that might affect the price of oil, such as the likelihood of certain political or military events in the future and the state of the world economy.

Determining probability is often a matter of 'best endeavours'. A fund manager who has a large amount of cash to invest will obtain all the information he can before deciding where to invest the funds. However, he will be cautious in telling investors the probable value of the fund at any time in the future and will point out to investors that any figures given are just estimates based on past and current performances and not a guarantee or contractual promise. There are too many variables outside his control to make definite predictions. He does not have a crystal ball – nor would investors be likely to be impressed were he to admit to using one.

In mathematics, the probability of an event is rated between 0 and 1. If some outcome is regarded as impossible the likelihood is 0, while an event that is considered certain will be rated as 1. It is not always quite that simple, as 'impossible' and 'certain' may not always be easy to define exactly. However, for our purposes, these numbers and terms are adequate. The main point here is that there is uncertainty involved and we want to determine, as far as possible, the magnitude of this uncertainty.

Take the example of tossing a coin. In this simple situation, there are just two possible outcomes – heads or tails. Probability tells us that the chance of heads coming up is 50% and the chance of tails coming up is also 50%. Therefore, in our 0-to-1 scale, the chances of heads or tails coming up are 0.5, or 50–50. The probability of it coming up both or neither is 0. This is the scientific view. A gambler, particularly a reckless one who cares little for probability, would be likely to take a different view. He believes in what could be called 'subjective' probability and believes that there is luck involved. When he believes that his luck is 'in', he will have a 'gut feeling' and be convinced that, say, heads will come up. And he might be right, for a while. If a fair coin is tossed 100 times and it comes up heads 60 times and tails 40 times, and our gambler had a 'gut feeling' for heads, then he wins. He has profited from a relative frequency of 0.6 and beaten the probability of 0.5 heads/tails. However, he would be well advised to quit while he is ahead, for, whether he accepts it or not, the probability of 0.5 heads/tails is still valid. If the gambler tosses the coin an infinite number of times, the probability is that it will come up heads 50% of the time and tails 50% of the time, based on the 0.5 probability. If the gambler has consistently bet heads or tails, the probability is that he will break even and have nothing to show for infinity.

Gamblers who believe in luck are capable of taking a very cavalier attitude towards the hard statistics of probability. When it comes to luck, gamblers, and indeed others as well, are able to accommodate most outcomes and fit them into their systems. For example, if tails comes up five times in succession then, depending on his mental processes and his interpretation of the five in a row, he may convince himself that the on the sixth toss it will also be heads. The coin is 'on a roll' and will come up tails again, he concludes. His friend, who has also seen the five in a row, but the conformation of whose mind is different, takes the opposite view, concluding that since the coin has comes up tails five times, heads is due. Sadly, they are both deluded, victims of fallacious thinking. The coin does not have a memory or know that it came up tails five times in succession. Those five tosses have no effect whatsoever on the outcome of the next toss. No matter what their 'gut feeling' or how 'lucky' they are feeling, the outcome of each toss is still 0.5 heads and 0.5 tails.

In roulette, with number from one to 36, plus 0 and 00, it is much more difficult, probably even impossible, to predict, in the case of a gambler betting on an individual number. The number of possible outcomes is now 38 rather than two. Before a gambler curses his luck for losing at roulette, it would be advisable for him or her to know the number of possible outcomes. However, what if the universe is deterministic, going about its business according to the laws of nature and Newtonian physics? If this is the case and a person, like our Prognosticator, knows all the conditions exactly, then maybe he can beat probability and predict what number will come up. In the case of roulette, if the gambler knows all about the force with which the wheel was turned, the speed of the ball when released, the strength of the forces of inertia and friction operating on the wheel and ball, the weight of the ball as well as its mass and smoothness, the temperature and humidity in the casino and every other possible variable, then the number on which the ball will stop can be predicted. The ball and wheel operate according to the laws of science, and these can be calculated. The probability of predicting the number on which the ball would stop would be 1, certainty. Lesser mortals, who do not have all this information, must put up with probability and the only solace that mathematics can offer them is that the probability of any particular number being a winner is 1 in 38. All this will, naturally, be irrelevant to a gambler who is 'feeling lucky' or has a 'gut feeling' that the ball will stop on a particular number. He does not give a hoot for probability.

In the case of dice, where there are six possible outcomes, it is more difficult to predict the outcome than with the coin toss, but less difficult than in the case of roulette. In dice, the chances that 1, 2, 3, 4, 5 or 6 will come up are simply 1 in 6. The probability that the number will be odd (1, 3 or 5) is 0.5 and the probability that it will be even (2, 4 or 6) is also 0.5. The probability that, say, 1 and 4 will come up is 0, impossible. As with the coin toss, were one to throw a die an infinite number of times, probability tells us that it would come up 1, 2, 3, 4, 5 and 6 an equal number of times. One could lose a large amount of money (an infinite amount!) gambling for infinity.

Coming to playing cards, the probabilities of certain outcomes are different again. In a deck of 52 shuffled cards, what are the odds, or probability, of picking out, say, a 10? As there are 52 cards in the pack and only four of them are 10s, the odds are 4 in 52, or 1 in 13. What if we wanted to pick out not just any 10 but the 10 of diamonds? As there is only one 10 of diamonds in the pack, the odds are 1 in 52. The chance of drawing a 10 or a diamond is 4, not 5, in 13 as one card is both a 10 and a diamond.

Now let's take the case of two people, each with a pack of cards. What is the probability that both of them will draw out the 10 of diamonds on their first try? The chances that the first person will draw out the 10 of diamonds are 1 in 52, and they are the same for the second person. The two draws are separate and independent, and the first draw does not affect the outcome of the second. When it is worked out mathematically, the chances that both will draw the 10 of diamonds are 0.00037, a very slim chance indeed. Of course, they might be 'lucky' and do it the first time, but it is hardly something one would bet on without getting exceptionally good odds. Again, bringing back our useful friend, infinity, if the two people persisted (or existed) that long, they would definitely (probability 1) do it some time. It might be sooner than one expected. Probability can be like that some times.

Every day people win large sums of cash in lotteries and beat probabilities that many would calculate as being close to 0. All holders of a ticket in a lottery or raffle have an equal chance of winning (or not winning). A person with more than one ticket obviously increases his or her chances of winning. In a lottery with 50 or 45 balls in the drum or bubble, the probability of any number coming out is 1 in 50 or 1 in 45. If your chosen numbers are, say, 3, 17, 24, 37, 40 and 44, what are your chances of getting all six if there are 50 balls in the drum? The chances of one of your numbers coming out first are 6 out of 50. Now there are 49 balls in the drum, so the chances of one of your numbers coming out are reduced to 5 out of 49. Put mathematically, the probability is $6/50 \times 5/49 \times 4/48 \times 3/47 \times 2/46 \times 1/45$. The odds of your having the six numbers that are selected out of the 50 are astronomical. But, you could be lucky!

Some gamblers place multiple wagers on horse-racing, dog-racing or some other competitive event, in such a way that the outcome of any one event determines their wager on subsequent events. This kind of bet is sometimes called an accumulator. Let's say you put down a double wager, for horse Number 4 to win the first race and horse Number 14 to win the second race. For you to win, both horses must win, or be placed, depending on the nature of your wager. This is not the same as placing two separate bets on horse Number 4 in the first race and horse Number 14 in the second race – these are two separate wagers and the outcome of one race does not affect your wager on the other. With the accumulator, it is different. The outcome of either race is not affected by the outcome of the other, but your wager is. It sounds like a good bet, because if your first horse wins, all your winnings are wagered on the second race. If both horses win, you win, but if either horse loses, you lose. Whether Number 4 wins or loses in the first race has no effect on the performance of horse Number 14 in the second race, but it has an effect on your wager. Obviously, in this accumulator wager, you will get better odds from a bookmaker than if you had placed two separate bets. The accumulator can be extended to cover three, four, five or whatever number of events. A gambler who engages in this kind of wager would be well advised to know the probability of his winning, or losing, and not curse his luck if he does not win. His potential winnings will reflect the likelihood, or unlikelihood, of his winning. This kind of wager can be very attractive to some gamblers, as the potential payout on a small initial wager can be significant if one wins, but it is a high-risk bet, as just one loss means all is lost. One could put it this way: if A, B, C, D and E all happen, then I will get X amount, but if any of A, B, C, D or E does not happen, I will get nothing.

But, you might ask, what about the professional gambler, the well-informed gambler who has studied the form and based his wager on the best information available? Certainly, he has a better chance of success than the gambler who sticks pins at random on the racing pages, or picks horses with 'lucky' names. However, no matter how the horse is chosen, probability and randomness still apply. Our professional has studied the form, the 'going' on the racetrack, the handicap if applicable and any other factor he can study. Despite all this, there is still a significant element of chance and risk. There are many things he does not know and which are outside his control. What if the ground conditions change suddenly or his selected horse is off-form, or the jockey has been given instructions to hold the horse back to increase its odds in its next race? There might be an accident. The horse might trip or fall at a jump. The horse might win the race but then be disqualified after a stewards' enquiry decides that the horse had unfairly impeded another runner, or there had been excessive use of the whip, or whatever. Even a professional gambler could not have foreseen these eventualities. Even the Prognosticator would have difficulty here.

Instead of betting on an accumulator, the gambler would have had a better chance of winning if he had bet on the horses individually, but the odds he would get would not be as good. His probability of selecting one winner out of two would be better than his chances of winning twice. As stated earlier, probability is not an exact science, as there is usually some randomness involved, such as the horse falling. While the universe may be deterministic, this does not mean that one can know with certainty what is going to happen. All this should be borne in mind by gamblers who blame their luck when they do not win.

Is the universe deterministic and operating according to Newton's Laws? Quantum mechanics has come up with situations in which it would appear that things are happening in a random manner. Some systems, while they may be deterministic, are so complex that it is impossible to predict what will happen. An example of this would be the movement of molecules in gases. If there is a lot of randomness, this does not help with predictability, as randomness, by its very nature, is unpredictable. Some scientists had trouble accepting randomness. In a letter to Max Born, Einstein wrote, 'I am convinced that God does not play dice'. Perhaps those who believe in luck would find it easier to accept the idea of randomness – that things happen by chance. At present, scientists are still working on this and many are now more inclined to ascribe probabilities to situations, conditions or outcomes, rather than making definite statements. However, those who work in the field of probability do not throw up their hands in despair and abandon their equations. While not denying that the unpredictable can occur, they try to put matters on a mathematical footing.

Let's assume that you drive to work every morning and the journey usually takes you 25 minutes. Consequently, you leave home at a certain time to get to work on time. You are assuming, or predicting, that it will take you roughly the same length of time to get to work today as it did yesterday. Now, let's introduce a little randomness. In the morning, you wake to find that there has been an unexpected snowstorm during the night. This means that it will probably take you longer to get to work. You will have to brush the snow off your car and, because of the more dangerous driving conditions, you will probably have to drive more slowly than usual. Consequently, you decide to leave for work a little earlier than usual. You have factored in the probable delay caused by the snow and given yourself more time to get to work. This can be called conditional probability and seems manageable enough.

Now, let's take a slightly different situation. It is a normal morning and you leave for work at your usual time but, unfortunately, your car breaks down –the engine stops, you have a flat tyre or a warning light flashes. This situation could not have been foreseen or planned for, particularly if your car was in good mechanical condition. What if, instead of a breakdown, you are delayed by an accident, oil spillage, gas leak, burst water pipe, police checkpoint or some other unexpected event? The end result is the same. You will likely be late getting to work, a victim of the unexpected. But while you cannot change the situation with which you are faced, you can, like the Stoics of old, choose how you react to it. You can curse your luck, honk the horn, shout obscenities, pound the steering wheel, make rude gestures at other motorists, or just sit patiently in your car waiting for traffic to move again. You may feel singled out for misfortune, not considering that all the other motorists around you are in the same situation. There are always choices, no matter what your perceived luck.

The likelihood of something happening or not happening is related to its frequency probability. In an experiment in which a scientist sets out to prove or disprove something, there are only two possible outcomes – he either succeeds or fails. If he does the experiment 1,000 times and it works out as true 900 times, then he has the frequency probability. This result may not hold up after further experimentation, but it is the situation as it is currently known. If the number of experiments carried out is very large, then it becomes more likely that the frequency probability can be more accurately assessed. This would be very useful for actuaries or others who are trying to predict likely or probable outcomes.

With chaotic or random systems, this would not be possible, as probability relates to how far a correct prediction can be made as to future conditions. With some systems, it is possible to predict their future or final states, but not with chaotic or random systems. In fact, such systems tend to become even less predictable as time goes on. But it is not entirely hopeless. Probability distribution attempts to quantify all the possibilities of a random variable. While the results will not be definite, they will, probably, be useful. In statistics, allowance is made for this and the degree of error is specified. Actually, in many branches of science, researchers are coming up with probabilistic rather than definite results, a range rather than a definite answer. This shows, as mentioned earlier, that certainty or impossibility (1 or 0) can be very difficult to determine, and we must be satisfied with the range of probabilities that lie between.

Those who believe in luck can interpret all this to support their belief. They can say that there is too much randomness and chaos about to accurately predict most things, so one might as well just depend on luck. One might think that were a gambler to know and admit to such randomness, he would be loath to gamble on such situations. This does not appear to be the case. At least with sporting events, there are a limited number of competitors. Team sport matches involve two teams, dog races usually six dogs and horse races seldom have more than 30 runners. There is past form to guide one. There is definitely room for skill and experience in deciding how to bet, and there is a wide variety of bets that can be made. Where the number of possible outcomes is very large, then luck (and probably also hope) becomes more significant factors. Not everyone who gambles may expect to win, especially in lotteries, but they all hope to win. Perhaps it is a combination of hope, belief in luck and an 'anyone can win' attitude that makes gambling such a popular pastime. For the price of a relatively cheap ticket, a person has a chance to win a huge sum of money. Surely, it is worth a try – you are at least in with a chance, though you might not like to be told just how probable (or improbable) are your chances of winning.

The probability of different outcomes can usually be calculated in most games, sporting events and other activities. We have seen that with a lottery, the probability is low, close to 0, but not impossible. Roulette gives the gambler a better probability of success (1 out of 38), dice a 1-in-6 chance of getting the number you want with a single die, and the coin toss a 50–50 chance. Of course, the greater the number of possible outcomes, the greater the potential winnings. Most people would agree that there is little or no skill involved in playing a lottery, dice or coin toss. It might be interesting to look at the probabilities, as well as the relative importance of luck or skill involved, in a number of other games and see how they compare.

Bridge is a card game with four players – two sets of partners. All 52 cards are in play. Teams bid the maximum they consider their cards are capable of making and the higher bidding team tries to make its 'contract'. After the bidding, one card is played and then one of the players of the team that is trying to make the contract puts his or her cards on the table, face up for everyone to see. This hand is called the 'dummy', as is the player who has put down his hand of cards. Then three players play out the game, the "dummy" player having no further input in the game. This is called contract bridge. Bridge is a game of skill where good players maximise the number of points which can be achieved by their combined hands. Cheating or bluffing are not factors in the game. But, you might say, some players were lucky, or unlucky, in the cards they were dealt. Let's accept that. Now we will eliminate this element of luck and turn to duplicate bridge. In this game, all the players in a bridge tournament take turns to play pre-dealt hands, at a number of tables, against all other teams. Each team tries to make the maximum number of points on each hand. The scores obtained by the players are noted and the winners of the tournament are the team with the most points. We will have to agree that in this case it was all skill, with no luck involved. The best team has won because they got the most points. The losers can hardly complain that the winner's success was due to good luck.

With poker, it is different. There are a number of variations of this game, such as stud, draw and the increasingly popular Texas Hold 'em. In draw poker, where all of a player's cards are hidden from his opponents, a person has few ways of knowing what cards the other players are holding. He may watch for what are called 'tells', which are expressions, gestures, tics or something else that a player tends to do when holding a good or bad hand. Good players are unlikely to have such 'tells', so they are not something that a professional player would count on too much. Basically, there is no way of telling, with a high probability of accuracy, what other players are holding. There is, of course, the old 'gut feeling', but this is very subjective and it might not be advisable to rely on it.

How can we determine how much is down to luck and how much is attributable to skill in poker? Is it all luck, just a matter of the cards one is dealt, or is skill a significant factor? Gamblers speak of 'short-term' luck, a period of time, usually quite short, during which a player may get a succession of good or bad hands. However, according to the theory of probability, if a number of gamblers play for an extended period, they will each get the same number of good, medium and weak hands. The luck evens out. Yet, some players win consistently while others regularly lose. The skilful poker player will know about the odds of the game. He or she will know the probability of getting certain hands, the odds of drawing a certain card and the chances of a particular hand winning a game. The unskilled player will not. The skilled player will lose less on weak hands and win more on strong hands, as he approaches poker as a game of money management. For most, or all, situations, he will have an optimum strategy, a way of proceeding that is the best in that particular situation. He will also know how to compare his chances of winning a 'pot' against how much he has to wager in order to stay in the game. He leaves as little as possible to chance and luck. However, it is not that simple. In poker the best hand does not always win, particularly in varieties of the game in which all a player's cards are hidden from his opponents. This is mainly due to what is called 'bluffing'. Here, a player with a weaker hand or a hand which he believes is probably not the best at the table bets in such a way to suggest a strong hand and confidence in winning. This show of betting may cause other players, some of whom may have stronger hands, to drop out of the game, thus allowing the bluffer to win. Bluffing can be a risky ploy as, if one is called, one is likely to lose. Other players will usually 'call' a player who they think may have a weak hand and who is known to bluff frequently.

In Texas Hold 'em, each player is dealt two cards, face down. Then at intervals, more cards are dealt face up in the middle of the table three, one and one at a time. These are common cards for all players who may use them to make their best five cards. In this game, the element of luck is reduced, as all players have equal 'luck' with the five cards in the middle, though they will be of more assistance to some players than others. Most of the luck is confined to the two face-down cards. 'Bluffing' is also less common but can be used to great effect on occasions. Here again, skill and experience will usually be the deciding factors in determining who wins or loses. The competent player will attribute little credit or blame to luck, relying instead on using his optimum strategy and playing each game on the merit of his cards.

In board games, such as draughts and chess, luck cannot be regarded as a significant factor. In each game, the players start with pieces in similar positions on the board. There is nothing hidden from one's opponent, except what one's moves will be, and cheating is not possible – so the player who wins must be counted the better player, not the luckier. Skill wins these games, not luck. Matters are somewhat different with board games in which a die or dice are used to determine the position on the board to which a player will move his playing piece or marker. In this situation, luck can be seen as playing a part, as there is chance or randomness in the throw of a die, unless one contends – as some will – that throwing dice is a skill. In Snakes and Ladders, most people will agree that it is a matter of chance whether one's piece lands on the bottom of a ladder or the head of a snake.

In craps, a player throws dice in an attempt to get certain numbers and not others. It is here that one is likely to find the individual who regards dice-throwing as a skill. Some players have certain rituals, such as blowing on the dice or rubbing them on the sleeve, which they perform before throwing, in the belief that this will improve their luck, or skill. It would not be surprising to learn that such players have taken the precaution of bringing along a rabbit's foot and/or a four-leaf clover to further enhance their luck. Sadly, for these individuals, the theory of probability still holds and the probability of rolling any particular number is a cold mathematical fact. Not knowing these facts, or choosing to ignore them, does not invalidate or disprove them.

Optimum Strategy

Optimum strategy simply means the best thing to do in a given situation. It is not always easy to determine the optimum strategy, particularly if one is not in possession of all the relevant information necessary to make an informed decision, or if there is time-related pressure. Still, one must make do with what one has, and make the best of it. To illustrate this, the following situation, or a similar one, is sometimes postulated.

Three men are involved in a truel (a duel involving three). Each has a duelling pistol. The order in which they will fire has been decided, based on their marksmanship. A is a very poor shot who hits his target only 25% of the time. B is better and hits his target 50% of the time, while C is a crack shot, hitting his target 100% of the time. As A is the inferior marksman, he is given the first shot. What should A do? What is his optimum strategy? Although it may seem counter-intuitive, A's optimum strategy is to fire into the air. Then it is B's turn to fire. He will likely shoot at C, as he is the best shot and therefore the most dangerous opponent. As B hits his target 50% of the time, there is a 50–50 chance he will hit C. If he hits C, then A now has a shot at B. If B misses C, then C is more likely to fire at B than A, as B is the better shot and, therefore, more of a threat. C will hit B and then A will have a shot at C. Had A decided initially to fire at B or C and had hit his target, the other man would have had a shot at A. Had A fired at B or C and missed, he would have gained nothing. Intuitively, one might have thought that A should have fired at B or C at first, but that would not have been his optimum strategy.

There are times when it is to the advantage of the individual to act cooperatively with others, to be a team player, in order to achieve his goals. On other occasions, it might seem to the individual that selfishness is his best option – to go it alone. In the case of a striker in soccer, there are times when he will pass the ball to a teammate who may be in a better position to score, but there are some attackers, who are sometimes referred to as 'hot-dogs', who are reluctant to give away possession of the ball if there is any chance of scoring themselves. They want the glory and adulation. Such players are often not popular with their teammates, or their managers, especially if their selfishness is believed to impair the overall performance of the team. It will depend on the situation, the mentality of the player and how often his style of play pays off. As most players want to be successful, popular and rich, they will probably do what they consider best in any given situation. They follow what they believe is their optimum strategy.

The game known as prisoner's dilemma is sometimes used to illustrate a situation in which an individual has to decide whether his optimum strategy is to act in a selfish or unselfish fashion, and where he also had to guess or predict what another person will do. In one version of the game, two men have been arrested and are being held in separate cells, awaiting questioning about the same offence. Then both A and B are given options. They are asked to confess. If neither of them confesses, they will be released, presumably because there is not enough evidence to detain them. In addition, they will each receive $500. If A confesses and B does not, A will be given $1,000, released and asked to testify against B at his trial. Similarly, if B confesses but not A, he will be given the same deal as A. If both confess, they will both be convicted, but will get reduced sentences. What should they do? Neither A nor B knows what the other will do. Can A rely on B not to confess and they will both go free with $500 each? Can B trust A to do likewise? Would taking this chance be their optimum strategy? If either A or B thinks that the other will confess, then his optimum strategy is to confess too. If either A or B decide not to confess, perhaps believing in honour among thieves, or criminals in general, and B confesses, then A is in a bad position. Maybe B is thinking in the same way. The optimum strategy for both A or B is to confess. It is the best way to avoid going to jail. While it is best for A or B to confess, it is not best for both of them, if both confess.

The scenario is interesting in that it has wider application in the world of commerce and in questions relating to the duties of the individual. It would apply to competitive situations and areas where the individual was expected to act for the good of society. It would also apply to contractors who have to make sealed bids for projects that are put out to tender, or to supermarket managers who have to decide how to price their goods.

It also applies to luck. If one's aim is always to do what he or she thinks most likely to ensure success, or at least avoid the worst, as far as possible, then the optimum strategy for a person who believes in the power of a rabbit's foot or four-leaf clover is to carry one at all times. It would be their optimum strategy. If these or other items were believed to bring good luck, then it would be foolish to be without them. The optimum strategy for primitive man living in a world of witchcraft would have been to observe all taboos, stay on good terms with everyone, and observe the usual norms of his society. To do otherwise would very likely lead to unfortunate results, which some might call bad luck. For the religious person who has a strong belief in God, the optimum strategy is to follow the rules of his religion and do what he believes God wants him to do, so as to please God and obtain blessings in this life and eternal reward in the next. To a person who does not subscribe to belief in either magic or religion, the behaviour of these people will seem strange or irrational, but he too will, no doubt, have his own optimum strategy, with which others may disagree.

People are different and there is much in life which is open to numerous interpretations. Each must find his path through life according to his beliefs and values. This is particularly true in an age of moral relativism in which one is cautioned against being judgemental and where one belief system is regarded as being as good as another, just different. Each to his own.

Newcomb's Paradox

A dilemma that is somewhat similar to that of the prisoners was put forward by William Newcomb of the University of California's Lawrence Livermore Laboratory. In this game, there is a Predictor (very like our Prognosticator), who is described by Newcomb as 'almost certainly' correct and in some tellings is described as being infallible.

A player is presented with two opaque boxes, which are marked A and B, by the Predictor. The player is asked to choose both boxes or just Box B. Inside Box A is $1,000. What is inside Box B is determined as follows. Before the game, the Predictor has predicted whether the player will take both boxes or only Box B. If he has predicted that the player will take both boxes, then Box B will have nothing inside. On the other hand, if the Predictor had foretold that the player will choose only Box B, $1,000,000 is put inside. This has been done before the player is asked to choose and, once the game has begun, the contents of the boxes cannot be changed. The player is aware of the rules, the fact that Box B may contain nothing or $1,000,000, and that this has been based on the 'almost certainly correct' prediction of the predictor. The player is not told what prediction has been made as to whether he will choose both boxes or Box B only.

What should the player do? What is his optimum strategy? The game is called a paradox as there are two strategies that both sound logical and rational, but will give different advice on which choice is likely to yield the bigger reward.

Strategy 1 – No matter what prediction has been made, taking both boxes is the better choice. If the prediction has been that both boxes would be chosen, then the player is choosing between getting $1,000 if he takes both boxes and nothing if he chooses only Box B. Taking both boxes sounds like his optimum strategy. If the prediction had been that the player would choose only Box B, he is still better off to take both boxes as, if he selects both he will get $1,001,000 while, if he selects only Box B, he will end up with $1,000 less.

Strategy 2 – The player should choose only Box B. In this case, the player will not get $0 or $1,001,000, as both of these sums would require the Predictor (who is 'almost certainly' right) to make an incorrect prediction. So the player has the choice of taking both boxes and getting $1,000 or just Box B with $1,000,000. Clearly, choosing Box B alone is the better decision.

In a 1969 essay titled *Newcomb's Problem and Two Principles of Choice*, Robert Nozick stated, 'To almost everyone, it is perfectly clear and obvious what should be done. The difficulty is that these people seem to divide almost equally on the problem, with large numbers thinking that the opposing half is just being silly.'

So what is the optimum strategy here? According to the Expected Utility Hypothesis, a player should expect more by choosing Box B, while the Dominance Principle would suggest that taking both boxes was the better decision, as one would expect to benefit more. Some argue reverse causation, thus leaving the player with no free will, so he is not really making a choice. This argument sounds weak, as free will is defined as being part of the situation. Others suggest that a rational, normal person will always choose both boxes, as the Predictor cannot really exist. But what if the Predictor could exist? If a person, or Being, has knowledge of the future, and this knowledge affects his actions and decisions, then future events will cause effects in the past. Causation is going backwards!

Game Theory

Game theory deals with the study of how a 'normal' person behaves in order to achieve his or her aims and objectives. It is used widely in the social sciences. It is of interest to psychologists, economists, sociologists and others. Social planners need to know as much as possible about human behaviour if they are to decide on an optimum strategy for the future. Game theory and optimum strategy are related and there will be areas in which the two overlap.

Game theory is an attempt to reduce to mathematical concepts the behaviour of individuals, societies, animals, plants and even computers. In the case of the individual, it studies how his decisions in making choices are affected by the behaviour of others. It attempts to identify strategies in which individuals are likely to behave in a certain, predictable way. It can also be extended to study how companies, states and consumers behave, as well as having applications in psychiatry, political science and philosophy.

In political science, rulers who want to know how people make choices use game theory. It is also used by candidates running for election who are keen to find out what policies should be presented to the public and how they should be presented to maximise their chances of being elected. In a broader sense, it is used in relations between states. There is a generally accepted view that democratic states are more open, more transparent and more trustworthy than non-democratic or 'rogue' states.

In dealing with states in which there is little or no democracy, there will be an element of suspicion and lack of trust and this will be reflected in what policies are adopted when dealing with these states. As Ronald Reagan used to say, 'Trust, but verify'.

In sociology, game theory is used to examine bargaining, distribution of wealth and how social groups are formed. It is also utilised in attempts to find out what 'normal' or 'rational' behaviour is and how individuals in groups behave in response to the behaviour of others. The general assumption is that individuals and groups will act in ways they consider beneficial. Philosophers are also interested in game theory. In their attempts to understand human beings, they try to determine how much of human thought and action is determined by self-interest and how much is due to altruism. This is important in considering the public interest.

Researchers have come up with a wide selection of games to test, or illustrate, various aspects of game theory. A useful way of looking at some of these games is to determine whether they are games of cooperation or non-cooperation. There is cooperation if players can form groups or teams (such as bridge partners) but there is no cooperation in a poker game, where it is one against all. Another way of classifying games is to consider whether the players have complete or incomplete information. In chess and draughts, the players have complete information while in poker there is incomplete information. Whether there is the completeness of information has a great effect on the decision process.

In games where there is complete information, luck is not usually regarded as being a significant factor, though this may be open to question. When a player's knowledge is not complete, but where skill and experience are important (such as in poker), it is not possible to rule out luck. With lotteries or scratch cards, where there is a complete lack of information and where experience or skill are not considerations, luck is regarded as playing a significant part.

Even in cases where there is complete information, it is not always easy to make a decision. In chess, where both players can see the position of all the pieces, each player has a great number of potential moves. The player must try not only to determine his optimum strategy but also to predict or anticipate his opponent's moves. Even in situations where the choice is a simple, binary, 'yes/no', 'do/don't' type of decision, it is not always easy.

Take the case of a young lady who has attended two job interviews and then finds herself in the fortunate position of being offered both jobs. Now she must decide, and there are time limitations. She has extensive, if not complete, knowledge of what both jobs offer and entail. She will use reason, logic and common sense in order to come to a decision. She will compare and contrast the salaries, terms and conditions of both jobs, the length of her commute to work, the potential for job satisfaction, chances of promotion or travel and anything else that she can think of which is pertinent to her decision. Despite all this, she may still find it difficult to decide and time is moving on. In such a situation, a person's decision may eventually come down to an emotional response, a feeling – a (much-maligned) 'gut feeling'. The Stoics sensibly tried to keep emotions out of the way as they believed that they impeded reason. If asked by a friend, our young lady might find it hard to explain why she had chosen one job rather than the other, but there is no doubt that emotions do play a part in decision making. A person might say, 'It felt right' or 'I had a feeling' to justify their decision. It seems that after all rational avenues have been explored, the emotions come into play – and may even have the final say in the matter. Some might say that her unconscious mind made the final decision. This might be where luck comes in or is believed to play a part. After all, luck is often spoken of as a feeling, such as 'feeling lucky'. Of course, there is no guarantee that the young lady has made the right decision and it is possible that she will never know for sure, because when she accepted one job offer, she automatically rejected the other. She will never know how things might have turned out had she taken the other job. That's how it is with 'the road not taken'!

There is also the other side of the coin, the devil's alternative, in which an unfortunate individual is faced with a choice in which both outcomes are unpleasant. Again, reason will be used to choose the less unpleasant eventuality, but there will also be an emotional input. A man who is trapped on a burning ship but is unable to swim will have to decide whether to stay on the ship and hope to be rescued, or jump into the water and take his chances. He may have only a short time in which to make his decision, or the fire will make it for him. In a developing situation like this, there will be other things happening that will have a bearing on his decision, or he might prefer to drown rather than burn to death. If he escapes, he will likely be called lucky.

In cases where only one individual in a group has survived a plane crash, shipwreck or some other catastrophe, it is natural to describe him or her as lucky. Some of these people feel that there has been some purpose, some big plan, behind their escape, that they have survived for some momentous reason. Many such people spend the rest of their lives looking or waiting for this reason to manifest itself, but are often disappointed. Their survival was just something in itself and must be taken as such. It was just their fate and it is debatable whether or not fate always has a purpose.

Some mathematicians and statisticians like to play with numbers and calculate the probability of certain events occurring. For some it might be calculating certain outcomes in card games, roulette or some other game of chance. For example, what are the odds of being dealt a hand of 13 spades at bridge? This has been worked out as about 1 in 635 billion, roughly 90 times the population of the world. Theory does not always work out in practice, but it is often the best we have to go on. The person who got the 13 spades would probably be called lucky. In fact, he would be no more so than people who had been dealt equally improbable hands.

An even more mind-boggling statistic was given on the quiz show 'QI'. Heralding a feat never before performed, Stephen Fry shuffled a pack of cards and declared:

> The chances that anyone has ever shuffled a pack of cards in the same way twice in the history of the world are infinitesimally small, statistically speaking. The number of possible permutations of 52 cards is '52 factorial' otherwise known as 52! or 52 shriek. This is 52 times 51 times 50 ... all the way down to one. Here's what that looks like:
>
> 80,658,175,170,943,878,571,660,636,856,403,766,975,289,505,440,883, 277,824,000,000,000,000.
>
> To give you an idea of how many that is, here is how long it would take to go through every possible permutation of cards. If every star in our galaxy had a trillion planets, each with a trillion people living on them, and each of these people has a trillion packs of cards and somehow they manage to make unique shuffles 1,000 times per second, and they'd been doing that since the Big Bang, they'd only just now be starting to repeat shuffles.

It is sometimes said that if enough monkeys were given enough typewriters (or word processors), one would produce the complete works of Shakespeare by chance. What is the probability of this happening? Let's say that there are 50 keys on a keyboard. As the monkeys are expected to faithfully produce the works of the Bard, there will have to be correct spelling, capitalisation, punctuation and spacing.

To begin with, all the letters, commas, spaces, capital letters, etc. in Shakespeare's complete works must be counted. Then select a six-letter word – let's say, 'Winter'. What are the chances of a monkey typing this word correctly? It has been calculated that the odds are about 1 in 15 billion. That is just for one word. Now imagine how long it would take to type all the plays and sonnets! It seems as if we may have to bring in our old acquaintance, infinity. Now we set an infinite number of monkeys in front of an infinite number of typewriters (or word processors) and give them an infinite amount of time to compete their assignment. With all these infinities, how could they fail, but one would not want to wait around to do the proofreading. However, perhaps the monkeys would be 'lucky' and finish their task in a relatively short time, or is luck confined to humans?

Let's consider this for a moment. Is a pampered dog luckier than a mongrel that has to scavenge for scraps? Is a caged animal luckier than its wild counterpart? It will likely lead a safer and longer life, but what about quality of life? Is a racehorse luckier than a draught horse? Is an Indian cow luckier than one on a dairy or beef farm in Europe? Is a plant that grows wild on a mountain luckier than one that grows on grazed land and is nipped in the bud? And what about inanimate objects? We have all heard of unlucky ships, cars and buildings. It is unlikely that there can be a definite answer that would satisfy everyone.

Any branch of science that deals with human behaviour is unlikely to be exact. People do not always act rationally – they can be unpredictable, selfish or altruistic. And in such situations it is very difficult, or even impossible, to come up with conclusions that could be called 'truth' or 'facts'. There are random acts of violence or altruism and one can be in the wrong place at the wrong time. One can also be in the right place when opportunity comes calling. Even the 'self-made' man will have to admit that he did not do it all on his own – that there were 'breaks' and situations where chance or the unexpected came to his aid.

Odds

Odds do not mean the same as probability, though they are often used as if synonymous. Were you to choose a month of the year at random, the *odds* that you will choose, say, October, are 1 in 11. The odds against your choosing October are 11 to 1. Here 11 represents the number of ways you can fail to choose October while

1 is the chance that you will. This is how the word 'odds' is used in statistics and probability theory. The *probability* of choosing October from the twelve months of the year is 1 in 12. Odds can be understood as relative probability and it is important that a gambler, particularly one who bets on horse and dog races, should be aware of the difference and how bookmakers utilise this.

Odds may be the most understandable way of telling a person what their winnings will be in the event of success. If you bet $5 at odds of 5 to 1 (5/1) and win, then you will get five times $5, which is $25, plus your stake of $5, making a total of $30.

The odds offered by a bookmaker may not be the real chances that something will or will not happen, but represent what he will pay on a winning outcome. As the bookmaker wishes to make a profit, the odds may not be as great as the probability or improbability of the outcome. The difference is sometimes referred to as 'the book'. In an event with four contestants, the real probabilities might be 40%, 35%, 15% and 10%, adding up to a total of 100%. The bookmaker may change these odds to 45%, 40%, 20% and 10%, making a total of 115%. This means that the book now has a profit (called over round) of 15. If the bookmaker is now careful and takes bets in the right proportion, he can make a profit of 30 by taking in 130 and paying out 100, including the initial stake. On the other hand, if a gambler can make bets when the odds of being paid more are greater than the real odds, then he should win. However, as there are so many variables in competitive events, theory and practice may not always work out the same.

Even the odds usually called 'evens' or 'even money' implies that it is 50–50 and that you can double your money. The probability is 50% or 0.5. This is not the way the word 'even' is used in gambling. If you bet $5 at even money and are successful, you will win $5 and get your stake back. If you then bet $5 at 4 to 1 (4/1), you will get $20 and your stake. This is better than evens, and this is how the bookmaker and experienced gambler understand it. In common usage, when referring to an event whose outcome is unknown, the phrase 'better than even' would be taken to mean that the probability of the outcome was greater than 50%.

If you were told that an event or outcome had an 80% probability, and another had a probability of 20%, then you would assume that the former is four times more likely to occur than the latter. What if you were given odds of 1 to 4 (1/4, or four to one on), on the 80% probability and odds of 4 to 1 (4/1) on the 20% probability? These might sound like fair odds, but in fact the odds of 4 to 1 on the 20% probability are sixteen times higher than the 1 to 4 on the 80% probability. It is in the gambler's financial interest that he should be familiar with the real odds he is being offered.

Gambling

Luck is probably more often associated with gambling than with any other activity in life and it is assumed by many that the operation of luck is more obvious in gambling than in most other situations. Gambling can be defined as any activity in which a wager is placed on the uncertain outcome of an event. There are many types of gambling. Wagers are placed on card games, bingo, table games, sporting events, electronic games, scratch cards, casino games and many others. You can make a bet with a friend on whether a statement is true or false. You can bet that something will happen (a back bet) or that something will not happen (a lay bet).

There are many different types of gambles and many different types of gamblers. There is the casual or infrequent gambler, who might have a 'flutter' on the Grand National or the Kentucky Derby, or an occasional scratch card or lottery ticket, just for fun and to have a little excitement and the possibility of winning. There is the professional gambler, who tries to make a living from gambling and is usually, or should be, well informed on all aspects of his particular type of gambling. He looks on it as a business and will not depend very much on luck. Then there are the compulsive gamblers. They are addicted to gambling and, unfortunately, many of them tend to rely on luck or 'feelings'. There have been studies showing that there are changes in the brain patterns of such people when they are gambling. This can lead to a psychological addiction, as can some drugs. With the addicted gambler, even if he or she continues to lose, they continue to gamble. This would seem to indicate that it is the act of gambling that hooks them, not the outcome. Such people get a 'rush' from gambling, like others get from cocaine, eating or some 'extreme' sport. Compulsive gambling can bring misery to those who are addicted as well as to their families and friends.

Most churches and religions are opposed to gambling and some prohibit it completely. In the past, many countries forbade gambling, but recently this has changed. In the United States, gambling is legal under Federal law, but each state may decide to prohibit or legalise it and how to regulate it. In Nevada, which has the famous gambling cities of Las Vegas and Reno, gambling has long been legal and some other US states are following this example. Macau, a former Portuguese colony not far from Hong Kong, was famous for gambling, as is Monaco. Gambling can be a very profitable enterprise and has been a significant source of revenue for some states.

The possible part played by luck in various gambling situations has been discussed earlier and attempts were made to determine how much was down to skill and how much to luck. It was concluded that, in situations in which there was a lot of randomness, luck might be seen as playing a major part, but in games where skill and/or experience were the deciding factors, luck could not be seen as significant. The matter is further complicated by the belief expressed by some gamblers that throwing dice or selecting numbers for a lottery or betting in roulette are skills, not random acts. In the same way, perhaps they believe that pulling the lever on a one-armed bandit is also a skill, and that, if done properly, the machine will pay out. In fact, as these machines are programmed to pay at random, it is a matter of when you pull the lever, not how.

When gambling with bookmakers or in a casino, it is important to remember that they have given themselves an 'edge', which is quite legitimate. Gambling is their business and if they do it properly, follow the rules and do not get too greedy, they will win and stay in business. Bookmakers and casino operators know much more about gambling than the average punter. They know the odds and the mathematics behind their business. They know how to win. In mathematical terms, the frequency of success multiplied by the amount bet is equal to the expected value. Being able to manipulate these variables in such a way that the outcome is positive is the secret of gambling success. Oh, and perhaps a little luck as well!

Randomness

Randomness refers to a process in which there does not appear to be any order, reason or cause. Early man, even with his strange ideas of cause and effect, must have noticed certain strange, inexplicable things and wondered 'why?' Despite this, it was not until the time of Fermat and Pascal that mathematics took an interest in the topic. In the physical sciences randomness has been detected in the movement of molecules, and quantum mechanics seems to suggest that there is a lot of randomness at the microscopic and sub-atomic levels.

Randomness is an elusive subject, but it would be wrong to think of it as incomprehensible or all bad. Randomness has played a vital part in biology. According to the Theory of Evolution, the great variety of life forms on the planet is due to natural selection. The theory postulates that there were random, genetic mutations in life forms. If a mutation made a life form more fit for survival, by being superior or better adapted, then that mutation was passed on in the gene pool. A mutation that resulted in an advantage in terms of survival or reproduction was passed on. On the other hand, if the mutation were to reduce the life form's chances of survival or reproduction, then the result could be extinction. The environment would also be a determining factor. The fact that the mutations were random can be interpreted as being a hit-or-miss, luck-of-the-draw type of situation. Forms that were favoured by the mutations were lucky while others were not, as the main goals of all life forms are to survive, breed and increase in number. That is the way with randomness – it favours some and not others.

Life forms themselves can act in a random fashion. The flight of a fly appears random, but it has a survival value, as it makes it more difficult for a predator to catch it. An animal such as an impala or hare, when being chased, will often make sudden, unpredictable changes of direction, in the hope of escaping their pursuers. The acts of throwing dice, spinning roulette wheels and shuffling cards introduce randomness, and indeed are intended to do so. As stated earlier, randomness is built into some electronic gaming machines, usually under the supervision and control of gaming boards. Drawing straws is a random way of selecting an individual for some task, often an unpleasant one. On other occasions the roll of a die, the toss of a coin or the turn of a card may be used to make a random selection. In cases like this, randomness is used to demonstrate that the decision is being made in a fair and impartial way with which no one can disagree. The matter is left up to luck. Although drawing straws or throwing a die are considered 'fair' ways of making such decisions or choices, the loser may complain that he has been unlucky.

Even in religion we find examples of divination or casting lots though, in general, religions prefer to see what some regard as randomness as the Will of God, or God moving in 'mysterious ways', or the exercise of free will. If people's actions are free, then they can also be regarded as unpredictable. From this, some would go on to argue that this disproves determinism, the idea that all things were set down at the beginning of time. Others will argue that human behaviour is not unpredictable. We fail to predict it, they argue, because the human brain is too complex to be fully understood. This gives rise to the notion that the human brain is too complicated to understand itself.

As we saw earlier, Martin Luther believed that man had little or no free will, but he was not prepared to grant very much randomness. God is free to do as He wishes, to choose to save or not save a person, and what He did was not random, though it might appear as such to ignorant humanity, who could not comprehend His will. Most Christian churches present a view of the world that is very deterministic and, hence, random events cannot occur. They believe the world and creation have a purpose and thus randomness cannot be allowed. We are back to Einstein's, 'God does not play dice'.

Randomness is related to complexity. When we think of complexity, we imagine something that is intricately arranged and has many parts. A complex system will exhibit variation, but is not random. In a 1948 paper in 'American Scientist' titled *Science and Complexity*, Warren Weaver divided complexity into Organised Complexity and Disorganised Complexity. In his view, with disorganised complexity (such as a system with millions of parts), the interaction of the parts may seem random but the properties of the system are not, and can be understood by the use of probability and statistical methods. With organised complexity, he believed that there were non-random and correlated interactions between the parts.

This would be of interest to a roulette player who has a 'system' and does not accept the idea of randomness. He will postulate that with the use of statistical methods and probability he can predict future winning numbers. While a roulette wheel with 38 possible outcomes is not considered particularly complex, and probability predicts that every number will win an equal number if times over infinity, that is hardly of much benefit to the mortal gambler who has to deal with the finite.

When it comes to luck, randomness is a significant factor. Gamblers who win at random games such as dice, coin toss or roulette will often credit their winning to luck. And they may be right, for a period. If they continue to play for an extended period, their luck is likely to change. With the coin toss, the likelihood is that they will break even but, with dice, at a 1 in 6 chance, they will likely lose. With roulette, it is even more likely that they will lose, the rewards of their short-term luck being eaten up by probability and randomness. As always, there can be exceptions.

Murphy's Law
This law states that 'Anything that can go wrong, will go wrong'. It is sometimes also known as Sod's law, possibly derived from the phrase, 'unlucky sod'.

There are a number of ways of interpreting this law. One view is that the universe is, somehow, perverse or even malign. Those who hold this opinion will point out that, if one drops a piece of buttered bread on the floor, the buttered side will, invariably, land face down. Another, more scientific view is that, if an experiment is performed numerous times, everything, including the unwanted, will occur. This would be in accord with probability.

Probably the earliest mention of such a law was by Alfred Holt in 1877. Addressing a group of civil engineers, Holt remarked: 'It is found that anything that can go wrong at sea generally does go wrong sooner or later ... The human factor cannot be safely ignored in planning machinery.' In this view some, at least, of what goes wrong is due to human fallibility rather than the universe being ill-disposed or antagonistic to humanity.

In 1908, the British magician Nevil Maskelyne wrote:

> It is an experience common to all men to find that, on any special occasion, such as the production of a magical effect for the first time in public, everything that *can* go wrong *will* go wrong. Whether we must attribute this to the malignity of matter or to the total depravity of inanimate things, whether the exciting cause is hurry, worry, or what not, the fact remains.

In *A History of Murphy's Law,* Nick T Spark attempts to determine who first came up with the term. Some contend that it was called after a development engineer, Captain Ed Murphy, though there is disagreement as to what he actually said. Probably the most generally accepted version is 'If there's more than one way to do a job, and one of those ways will result in disaster, then somebody will do it that way'. Here again we find human fallibility as being the main reason why things go wrong.

Those who have a strong belief in luck, or think that they are dogged by ill-fortune, will probably be more inclined to the malevolent universe interpretation. There is no doubt that most people will, on occasion, blame on ill-fortune something that is actually their own fault. However, there are times when it is very easy to blame luck, or the universe, for the evils that befall us. As Robert Burns wrote, 'The best-laid schemes o' mice an' men / Gang aft a-gley'.

The Man Who Broke the Bank at Monte Carlo

As I walk along the Bois Boolong
With an independent air
You can hear the girls declare
'He must be a Millionaire'.
You can hear them sigh and wish to die,
You can see them wink the other eye
At the man who broke the bank at Monte Carlo.

Many people have heard the song *The Man Who Broke the Bank at Monte Carlo*, part of whose lyrics appear above. It was written in 1892 by Fred Gilbert about the gambling activities of a man named Charles Deville Wells (1841–1922), who had won a significant amount of money in Monte Carlo, Monaco, in 1891.

With £4,000 which he had obtained by fraudulent means, Wells arrived in Monte Carlo in July 1891. In a session lasting eleven hours, he broke the bank twelve times and won a million francs (about £4 million today). In France of the 1890s, the phrase 'break the bank' did not mean that a gambler had taken all the casino's cash. A gambler was said to have 'broken the bank' if he or she won more than the chips at the table. The phrase used was *faire sauter la banque*, which can be literally translated as 'blow up the bank'. When this happened, a black cloth resembling a shroud was draped over the table.

During the eleven hours of play, Wells had some remarkable runs. In one case, out of 30 spins of the wheel, he won 23 times. He took his million francs and left Monte Carlo. Four months later, he returned. This time he won a million francs in three days. Again, there were some amazing runs. He put money on the number 5 on five consecutive occasions, and won every time. The casino owners were, naturally, suspicious and hired detectives to keep an eye on Wells. The detectives found out nothing. According to Wells, there was no system or cheating involved. He said that he had just been lucky.

Because of his success, he became something of a celebrity and the popular song was written about him. Wells could not resist cashing in on his fame. He put out word that he was an accomplished engineer and inventor. He claimed to have invented a gadget that would reduce fuel consumption in steam ships. With the money he obtained from hopeful, but gullible, investors, he returned to Monte Carlo in 1892. He travelled on a splendid yacht (which was supposedly testing his fuel-saving device) and was accompanied by his mistress. He hit the tables again and broke the bank six times before his luck changed. Then he proceeded to lose all his money as well as that of the investors. Shortly after this, the law caught up with him. He was arrested at Le Havre and extradited to England to stand trial on a charge of fraud. He was found guilty and sentenced to eight years in prison. After his release, he was again convicted of fraud and sentenced to three years' imprisonment. Wells emigrated to France, but he still could not stay out of jail. He was sentenced to five years for fraudulent financial transactions. He died a poor man in Paris in 1926.

When one talks about a man breaking the bank at Monte Carlo, one might also be referring to Joseph Hobson Jagger (sometimes spelt Jaggers). Some even claim that he was the inspiration for the song. However, as his win took place in 1875 and the song was not written until 1892, Wells' win of 1891 is the more likely inspiration.

Jagger was born in September 1829 in Shelf, a small village near Halifax in Yorkshire. He worked as a mechanic in the local cotton industry. With his mechanical background, he began to think about roulette wheels. He thought that if a roulette wheel were not perfectly balanced and did not run true, then the numbers that came up would not be totally random. Jagger went on to win the modern equivalent of about £3.5 million. How did he do it? Was he lucky? Did he have a system? Well, a bit of both!

Jagger hired six people to note the numbers that came up at six roulette wheels at the Casino at Monte Carlo. From this, he learned that one of the six wheels seemed to have an unusually high occurrence of nine numbers (7, 8, 9, 17, 18, 19, 22, 28 and 29.). These numbers seemed to come up more frequently than the theory of probability would have predicted. On 7 July 1875, Jagger began to gamble on this particular roulette wheel. Before long, he had won £14,000 (the equivalent of about £700,000 today). He gambled for three days and brought his winnings up to £60,000. Other gamblers began to bet on Jagger's numbers and the casino was losing a fortune. In order to stop this winning streak, it relocated the six roulette wheels. Jagger continued to gamble, but now lost steadily. After a while, he noticed that a small scratch that he had seen on his winning wheel was no longer visible. He checked out the other wheels and located his winning wheel with the scratch. He continued gambling and winning. The casino management changed the metal dividers between the numbers every day in a further attempt to end their losing streak. Jagger continued to gamble for two more days but lost. He decided to quit. He had won around £65,000 (about £3,500,000 today). He left Monte Carlo and never returned. He left his job in the cotton mill and invested his money in property. He died in 1892.

Those who believe in luck are often castigated by non-believers for being superstitious, naïve or even stupid. Such a general statement would be impossible to prove and is probably prejudiced. Intelligence and luck, or the lack of both, are seldom connected. However, there comes a point when a person who blindly believes in their luck and engages in long odds or random bets will lose – not just the odds but also randomness and unpredictability are against him. Many addicted gamblers engage in subjective and fallacious thinking, which distorts the true picture and justifies their continued gambling. Say a person has been laying money on the roulette table on number 7 for 20 minutes. The number has not come up once in these 20 minutes so he 'reasons' that it must come up soon and continues betting on it. Of course, the number 7 will come up some time, but by then he may have lost his chips. Having lost all his chips on 7, he may now conclude that 7 is actually an unlucky number and, when he has money to gamble again, will pick another number. He does not realise that in roulette, all numbers have an equal chance of coming up, and no numbers can be proved, mathematically, to be lucky or unlucky. The gambler who does not realise or accept this is being deluded by a logical fallacy. The roulette wheel, ball and numbers have no memory. The only one keeping count is the gambler. With such a system of 'lucky' numbers, a gambler could end up with a small fortune – that is if he started with a large fortune.

The situation is similar if one is asked to pick, say, the four of spades from a pack of 52 cards. You draw a card and it is not the four of spades. You then return the drawn card to the pack, shuffle it and draw again. Now the odd of drawing the four of spades are the same again, that is 1 in 52. But if, instead of returning the drawn card to the pack, you take it out and try again for the four of spades, your chances are slightly better, 1 in 51. As the number of cards in the deck decreases, the chances of selecting the four of spades increase. There is no system here, just probability. This, however, does not stop some gamblers from coming up with 'systems'. Say the number 25 has come up three times in the last 20 turns of the roulette wheel. One gambler will base his 'system' on this to predict that the number 25 is 'hot' and will come up again very shortly. Another gambler might deduce that, because 25 has come up so many times in the last 20 turns, it will not come up again for a long time. It all comes down to a failure to understand probability and randomness.

While randomness is not the same as unpredictability or chaos (as will be explained later), there is no way of foretelling the outcome of a random event. A fly is sitting in the centre of a circle that has been divided into 360 degrees. Can you predict what bearing it will take when it flies off? No, but that does not mean that some people will not bet on it, and probably consider themselves unlucky if they do not win.

Apart from gambling and evolution, randomness has implications in many other areas of life. Volcanologists are concerned by a super-volcano that lies under Yellowstone National Park in Wyoming. They know that it will erupt at some point in the future, with devastating consequences, but they do not know when. They know it has erupted in the past and could go up again tomorrow, next year, or thousands of years in the future. Despite their best efforts and most sophisticated equipment, they do not know when. It is the same with other less massive volcanoes around the world. Seismologists expect that one day there will be a major earthquake along the San Andreas Fault in the western United States, but again, they do not know when. Volcanologists and seismologists are doing everything they can to make their science more exact but they are faced by randomness and variables over which they have no control. The best they can do is deal in probabilities, not certainties. Often there is very little advance warning of volcanic eruptions, earthquakes, tsunamis or other natural disasters and people have no time to evacuate or prepare for what is coming. Were it possible to predict such natural disasters, many lives could be saved.

As stated earlier, randomness is not the same as unpredictability or chaos. While it is true that random processes are not perceived as following any pattern that can be determined, they do follow a probability distribution. Chaos, on the other hand, is generally understood to mean the total lack of order. This is not the meaning given to the word in scientific use. Chaos theory is concerned with the behaviour of certain dynamical systems (systems which evolve and change with time) that are determined by, and highly sensitive to, the initial condition of the system. While the behaviour of a system that is called chaotic may appear to be random, it is in fact deterministic, as the initial condition has determined and defined its future dynamics. This, however, does not mean that we can fully understand the system.

Aleatory

'Aleatory' comes from the Latin *alea* and means 'depending on the rolling of a die'. The rolling of a die or dice is often used to introduce randomness for the purpose of gambling or otherwise. Robert Burns' lines quoted at the beginning of this chapter often seem appropriate to life, and it is understandable that there are occasions when one may be tempted to throw up one's hands and let luck, destiny, fate or whatever just take its course. In his novel *The Dice Man*, Luke Rhinehart has his hero make decisions based on the roll of dice. The music of John Cage could be called aleatory in its secondary meaning, or indeterminate, as chance is utilised in its composition. Andy Voda's 1979 movie *Chance Chants* relied on chance outcomes such as selecting a number at random or flipping a coin in making creative decisions. The movie *SN* by Fred Camper, made in 1984 but not screened until 18 years later, ended up as 18 reels of film. The toss of a coin was used to select three of those 18 reels for showing and even the order in which these were to be shown was decided by a coin toss. This meant that Camper could have ended up with 4,896 different movies. The 1971 six-reel film *Permutations* (full title *Six Reels of Film to be Shown in Any Order*) by Barry Salt could have been any of 720 different movies, depending on the outcome of the projectionist's roll of the die supplied with the film.

The human brain dislikes randomness, unpredictability and things that do not follow a logical, rational or predictable order. The brain is a wonderful patterning machine that will try to find patterns and impose order on whatever input with which it is presented. It likes to put things in groups, such as A, B, C, D or 1, 2, 3, 4. If two images or stimuli enter the brain at the same time, or in very close proximity, it will try to find some connection between them. If there is no obvious pattern, the brain will often try to impose or generate one. While the survival potential of such behaviour is significant, it can lead to strange bedfellows. Were a person to watch any version of Voda's or Salt's movies, their brain would try to find sequences, connections, themes, patterns or anything else that might 'make sense' of what it is being presented. The brain likes to get clear, unambiguous messages that can be analysed quickly and a response formulated. These abilities are very useful when being chased by a lion or in any situation where one is in imminent danger and a quick decision has to be made. The brain quickly analyses the information and decides on an appropriate response, such as fight or flight. But what if the brain is receiving conflicting messages? Put your right hand in warm water and your left hand in cold water and what will the brain make of it?

This organising and patterning behaviour of the brain has implications for luck and gambling. The compulsive or non-professional gambler can use – or more correctly, misuse – this behaviour to associate or combine things that would not usually go together. He can even convince himself that what he is doing is rational and explicable and therefore likely to lead to success. The 'thinking' goes something like this. The last time he wore red socks he won and the last time he took a bus rather than drove to the racetrack he was successful in his bets. It would be foolhardy for them not to repeat such winning behaviour. To them, there appeared to be a pattern, a cause-and-effect situation. It worked in the past, so why should it not also work in the future? The brain of the addicted gambler, when in the throes of his passion, would, if scanned, show very different patterns of activity than if he were eating his breakfast or putting on his shoes. When it comes to the stage that he can 'feel' a win coming on, or when he has convinced himself that he has put his spell of rotten luck behind him, it is unlikely that he would appreciate or listen to a lecture from a well-meaning friend on probability, randomness or unpredictability.

People have a great ability to see what they want to see, or believe what they want to believe. Faith is in operation not only in religion but also in many other areas of life. While all 'normal' people are able to reason and use common sense, this does not mean that they use these faculties all the time. People may have beliefs, feelings or prejudices which they know, deep down, are irrational, but which they are unable to change. It is all part of being in one's comfort zone and a person does not like to be ejected from there into the cold world of uncertainty and doubt. Some psychologists say that people become addicted to their beliefs and opinions and find it as difficult to change them as it is for a heavy smoker to give up cigarettes or an alcoholic to stop drinking. In addition, how much is physical and how much psychological is not always easy to determine, as there is no clear dividing line between the two.

The story is told of an African farmer who could not find his axe, one of his few worldly possessions. He looked long and hard for it, but without success. Then he concluded that his axe had been stolen – and he knew just who had stolen it! The thief was the teenage son of a neighbouring farmer. Yes, there was no doubt the teenager was the culprit. Didn't he have a sly, devious look, quiet and sneaky, unwilling to make eye contact and untrustworthy? There could be no doubt of his guilt. The farmer thought hard, trying to decide what to do. Maybe he should confront the teenager or his father, or perhaps he should think more about it before accosting them. The father would no doubt defend his thieving son. For some time thoughts such as these ran through the farmer's mind. He was having difficulty deciding what to do. What about visiting a witchdoctor for advice and assistance? Four days later the man's wife came to him with his axe. Although he was happy to see his axe, he could not fail to see she was in a bad mood.

'What did you think you were doing, hiding the axe in the roof of our hut?' she demanded. 'It could have fallen on someone and killed them.'

Then the farmer remembered. He had put the axe up there about a week earlier to have it out of the reach of his young son, whom he had found playing with it. He was happy to have his precious axe back. Luckily, it had not been stolen – he might never have seen it again! So, the teenager had not stolen the axe after all, despite his deviousness and shiftiness. It was lucky the farmer had not accused him of the theft. What would have happened if he had? What would the teenager or his father have done? Perhaps they would have gone to a witchdoctor to get revenge on him.

Now the farmer began to feel a mixture of fear and relief. He had been wrong about the teenager and before long began to see him in a different light. It was not slyness but shyness that showed on the young man's face, he thought. The look that seemed to be devious and furtive was just bashfulness and respect for his elders. The teenager was, he mused, a well-behaved young fellow who was polite, obeyed his father and was a diligent worker. How could he ever have suspected him of stealing his axe?

The farmer had learned from his experience. The gambler and blind believer in luck often do not. One would think that after a run of losses it might be sensible and prudent for the gambler to give up and find another avocation. But no, the losses, which he interprets as a run of bad luck, just mean that he is due a run of good luck and he must continue to gamble so as to cash in on it. It would be foolish to stop now, just as his luck was about to change.

Chapter 6

Luck and Coincidence

In the field of observation, chance favours the prepared mind.
Louis Pasteur

Men of action are favoured by the Goddess of luck.
George S Classon

Luck is the by-product of busting your fanny.
Don Sutton

Stemming from the Latin *co* (which could be translated as 'with', 'together' or 'in') and *incidere* ('to fall on'), 'coincidence' can be taken to mean things that fall together without any apparent reason. The word 'apparent' is used here, as there may be causal relationships between two events that are not immediately obvious.

Many coincidences are less surprising than might at first seem likely, and in statistics coincidence is treated as inevitable. As with many things in life, there are numerous views on coincidence. Many scientists hold the opinion that most people who claim that certain events are coincidences are merely failing to see or understand the cause-and-effect relationship between the two events in question, or are making false associations. As we saw earlier, the human brain is very good at connecting things that may or may not be connected in reality, especially if both messages enter the brain at or about the same time. In this context, it could be said that it is the mind, not external reality, that creates the coincidence. Deepak Chopra and others who work in the field of Vedic and mystical teachings believe that there is no such thing as coincidence because everything that happens must be the result of some earlier cause. Recent work in mathematics and physics (non-locality theory) seems to support this view. Others, however – particularly Carl Gustav Jung and Charles Fort – believed otherwise and have published accounts of an impressive number of coincidences to support their hypotheses. There are those who regard coincidences as pathways to, or messages from, the world of the paranormal. A belief in predestination or fatalism would support acceptance of coincidence as a valid phenomenon, as it would be the playing out of pre-planned, inevitable events.

Luck is often associated with coincidence, especially when the latter is seen as the result of determinism or fate. The attitude is that what happens was meant to be, and that is taken to mean that things are outside the control of humans. This belief will be especially strong in gamblers who engage in wagers where there is large degree of randomness, such as bingo, lotteries, scratch cards and roulette. If unlikely coincidences take place, they reason, then why should a win in the lottery not happen too? This is not to say that most people regard winning as a coincidence, but that unlikely and strange coincidences prove to them that luck and chance are significant forces in the world, perhaps even the universe. Those who regard themselves as unlucky will often think or say, 'the world is against me'.

Gamblers – even those who engage in games where the chances of a win are very low, due to randomness and the large number of possible outcomes – would be well advised to know something about the odds they are up against before they start cursing or crediting their luck. Were they to realise the true odds they are fighting against, as stated earlier, it might discourage them or 'bring them to their senses'. Reality is real, and not knowing the odds against one does not improve them, no matter how convoluted or tortuous the thought processes of certain gamblers.

It is the same with coincidence. It is useful to know the odds, the likelihood or unlikelihood of two or more coincidental events occurring. What is first regarded as 'a weird coincidence' may not, on closer examination, be so unlikely or coincidental at all. If you were asked how many people you would have to gather together to ensure that two of them had the same birthday, what would you say? You might do a quick mental calculation, telling yourself there are 365 days in a year and if a person is born on a certain day, then there are 364 days on which he or she was not born, but on which others could have been born. At this point, you might try dividing, adding or otherwise manipulating numbers in your head. You have a feeling that it will be a pretty large number, but cannot work it out exactly.

'Oh, I dunno,' you say, 'maybe a few hundred.'

The actual answer would then be likely to surprise you. With only 23 people in a group, the chances that two of them share a birthday are 50% or 0.5!

You might exclaim, 'What a coincidence', and muse on it for a bit. Then you ask, 'So, if there were twice as many people, the chances would be 100%? Who would have thought it?' Actually, with 46 people you get a 95% chance and with 57 the chances rise to 99%.

Many people have heard of the seemingly amazing number of coincidences between presidents Abraham Lincoln and John F Kennedy. Both were assassinated on a Friday and, in both cases, their wives were present. The words Kennedy and Lincoln both have seven letters and there are fifteen letters in the names of both assassins, John Wilkes Booth and Lee Harvey Oswald. Both presidents were shot in the head. Oswald shot at Kennedy from a warehouse (the book depository) and then ran to hide in a cinema (or theatre), while Booth shot Lincoln in a theatre and ran to a shed (where, it is said, a horse had been left to facilitate his escape). Lincoln was shot in the Ford Theatre, Kennedy in a car made by a Ford subsidiary (Lincoln). Lincoln was succeeded by a southerner named Andrew Johnson, while Kennedy was succeeded by a southerner called Lyndon Johnson, both of whom have thirteen letters in their names and were born exactly 100 years apart, Andrew in 1808 and Lyndon in 1908. Lincoln and Kennedy were elected to office 100 years apart.

This list of coincidences sounds impressive and might incline one to believe in 'weird' coincidences – but it is only one side of the story. If one were to work through masses of random data, similarities, or what appear to be coincidences, would be found. Let us look at the other side of the coin. Granted that there were many similarities in events and dates relating to Lincoln and Kennedy, what about the differences? Kennedy was born into a rich family in Massachusetts, Lincoln in a log-cabin in Kentucky. Lincoln was shot from point-blank range with a pistol, Kennedy from a distance with a rifle. Lincoln was sitting still when shot, Kennedy was moving in an open car. No one else was injured by gunfire when Lincoln was assassinated (though Booth injured his ankle when he jumped from the balcony on to the stage), but in the Kennedy assassination, Governor John Connally of Texas, who was sitting beside him, was seriously injured. Lincoln was killed in Washington DC, Kennedy in Dallas, Texas, thousands of miles to the west. Lincoln and Kennedy were born on different dates and days. They were not the same age when killed. One could go on and note down hundreds of dissimilarities between the two men and the circumstances surrounding their deaths.

While on the subject of United States presidents, let's look at some of them from the other end of the life cycle. Of the first 41 presidents, how many were born on the same date? Dealing with birthdays earlier, we saw that with 46 people there was a 95% probability that two of them would share a birthday. How about with 41? Actually, of the 41 presidents in question, two were born on the same date – Warren G Harding and James J Polk shared a birthday on 2 November. What about presidents (not necessarily still in office) who died on the same date? Would the probabilities be the same? Millard Fillmore and William Howard Taft both died on 8 March. What if one were to push it a lot further and ask what were the chances of two presidents dying not just on the same date but on the same day? Thomas Jefferson and John Adams both died on 4 July 1826 – exactly 50 years after they had signed the Declaration of Independence. Only one president, Calvin Coolidge, was born on 4 July. Are all of these coincidences?

As we saw earlier, with just 23 people, there is a 50% chance that two of them will have the same birthday. In that case, we were just looking for people with birthdays on the same date, without specifying a particular date. Were we to specify a date, say 11 February, how many people would we need in our group to have a 50% chance that two of them were born on that date? The answer is 613. To have a 50% chance of finding just one person with the specified birthday, we would need 253 people. What this shows is that a particular, specified event is much more unlikely than one which is not narrowly specified. In other words, many events that would generally be regarded as improbable are, in fact, quite likely. If we keep this in mind, it might alter our attitudes to coincidences and luck. But no matter how analytical, statistical, mathematical, logical or rational we get about coincidences (and luck), they are still fascinating and we feel that there is something beyond the dry numbers and pedantic statements.

People who find coincidences are often looking for them and even 'cherry pick' events that suit them, while ignoring those that do not. This in itself does not disprove that coincidences occur, but it does show the situation in a different light. If we believe that we have experienced a coincidence, we marvel at it, tell others and wonder if there is some significance behind it. You had a dream about a person you had not seen for years and, the following day, run into them in the street. What a coincidence! It would be churlish to ask this person how many people they had dreamt of over the years and not run into afterwards. As the Bard said, 'We are such stuff as dreams are made of', and Yeats asked us to 'tread softly because you tread on my dreams'. Why slit a blackbird's throat to find out what makes it sing so sweetly?

Remarkable Coincidences

James Dean's car
James Dean was a popular Hollywood actor, famous for such movies as *Rebel Without a Cause*, *East of Eden* and *Giant*. He was killed in September 1955 while driving his Porsche sports car. The wrecked car was towed to a garage where the engine fell out and broke both legs of a mechanic. The engine was later bought by a doctor who was interested in car racing. He had the engine installed in his car and not long afterwards was killed during a race, along with another driver. That driver's car had the driveshaft from Dean's car in it.

Although Dean's car was badly damaged, because of its fame (or notoriety) it was repaired. The garage in which it had been repaired burned down. When the famous car was put on show in Sacramento, California, it dropped off its mounts. An unfortunate teenager, who happened to be in the wrong place at the wrong time, sustained a broken hip.

As the car was being towed through Oregon, the trailer on which it was being transported came away from the tow-bar and crashed into a shop. Eventually, four years after Dean's fatal accident, in 1959, the car dropped off its metal supports into eleven pieces. Was it a 'bad-luck' car?

Twin deaths
In 2002, a 72-year-old man was killed by a car while riding his bicycle on a road in

Raahe, northern Finland, about 600 kilometres (370 miles) from Helsinki. Two hours later another 72-year-old man was killed on the same road, about 1.5 kilometres (just under a mile) from where the first man had been killed. The men were twin brothers.

Brothers killed a year apart
In 1976, a man was riding a moped in Bermuda and was struck by a taxi and killed.
   In 1977, a man was riding a moped in Bermuda and was struck by a taxi and killed.
   The two men were brothers. At the time of their deaths, they had been riding the same moped. They had been killed by the same taxicab, driven by the same taxi driver. On both occasions, there had been one passenger in the taxi. On both occasions it was the same passenger.

A bullet with his number on it
In 1883, a man called Henry Ziegland broke off his relationship with his fiancée. The distraught young lady committed suicide. Her brother blamed Ziegland for her death and decided to deal with him. He found Ziegland and shot him. Then he shot himself. What he was not to know was that he had not killed Ziegland. The bullet had merely creased his face and embedded itself in a tree.
   A number of years later, Ziegland decided to cut down the tree, the bullet still buried in it. As the tree was rather large, he decided to use dynamite to blow it up. The force of the explosion drove the bullet out of the tree directly at Ziegland's head, killing him.

Poker winners and losers
In 1858, a gambler named Robert Fallon won a poker pot of $600. A dispute broke out, as it was claimed that he had cheated. The row ended in Fallon being shot dead. The $600 lay unclaimed on the table, as none of the other gamblers would take it because they regarded it as unlucky. However, they did not let this disturb their game too much. They continued to play, with a vacant chair at the table. After a while, a player was found for the vacant chair and he was given the $600 as a stake. By the time the police arrived, the $600 had become $2,200. The police asked for the $600 to give to the next of kin. They did not have far to look for the next of kin. The player who had taken Fallon's chair (and the $600) was his son, who had last seen his father seven years previously.

King Louis XVI and the 21st
As a child, Louis had been warned by an astrologer to be particularly careful on the 21st of each month. He took the warning seriously and did very little on that day. Louis was a somewhat reluctant king and would have been happier just to take life easy and work on old clocks. He was unfortunate in that he was in the wrong place at the wrong time. In 1789, the French Revolution broke out. For three years, Louis XVI and his wife, Marie Antoinette lived a rather dangerous and precarious existence. Eventually, on 21 June 1791 they tried to escape from France but were arrested in Varennes. On 21 September 1791, the institution of the monarchy was abolished. A republic was proclaimed, based on the principles of Liberty, Equality and Fraternity. Louis was now surplus to requirements and on 21 January 1793, he was guillotined.

The King and the restaurant owner
King Umberto I of Italy went to a small restaurant in Monza along with his aide-de-camp, General Emilio Ponzia-Vaglia. They were waited on by the restaurant owner. The king remarked on the striking resemblance between himself and their waiter. The two men were almost identical, both facially and in stature. That was not all they had in common. Both had been born on 14 March 1844. Both were married to a woman named Margherita. The restaurant owner had opened his business on the day Umberto had been crowned king.

On 29 July 1900, King Umberto I received news that the restaurateur had died earlier that day in a strange shooting accident. While the king was expressing his sadness over the man's death, he was assassinated by an anarchist.

Synchronicity

Synchronicity is the occurrence of two things that happen in what is (or is interpreted as being) a meaningful way and which do not appear to be linked by cause and effect. It is not an attempt to disprove cause/effect – and attempts to do so would be seen by many as absurd – but rather to link events by means other than causality.

Some hold the view that the mind is configured in such a manner that, when conceptualising ideas, it may generate relationships that are not causal, in the usual sense of the word, as cause and effect are said to occur simultaneously.

The word 'synchronicity' was coined by Carl Jung for what he variously termed 'temporally coincident occurrences of acausal events' and 'an acausal connecting principle' or a 'meaningful coincidence'. In the scientific world, there are many who say that Jung was practising what psychologists call 'confirmation bias'. This means that he sought any information that might seem to support his hypothesis or theory of synchronicity, while ignoring anything that might appear to prove otherwise. This 'cherry picking' – taking what you want and ignoring all the rest – is hardly sound scientific method.

The power of the mind to look for and find patterns and connections was mentioned earlier, and this has been put forward by some as an explanation for synchronicity. Significance is given to events which may not, in fact, have any. This is known as apophenia. Synchronicity, in most cases, seems to happen in the mind but it would be difficult, if not impossible, to test this in the laboratory. This, in itself, does not invalidate the concept, any more than absence of proof is proof of absence. When one considers all the things that can and do happen in the course of a person's lifetime, it is likely that there will be events that are, or can be interpreted as, 'meaningful coincidences'. This is one viewpoint.

Findings in chaos theory, fractal geometry and quantum physics, some of them quite recent and in the early stages of development, seem to suggest that there are hidden, or undetected, connections between atoms, cells and molecules – between man and the natural world. There is an exchange of information between them that cannot be qualified or quantified. In an experiment involving two photons, physicists found that when the two were separated, by however great a distance, whatever change took place in one photon immediately happened in the other. It even seems that the information transfer between the photons, if such it is, happens at a speed greater than that of light.

Another view is that enshrined in the saying, 'Synchronicity happens when God wishes to remain anonymous'. Some people, who are spiritually inclined, regard synchronicity as the connection, or connecting principle, between the inner world of the mind and the outer world of perceived reality. In this case, synchronicity is often associated with intuition and the feeling that there is 'something out there' which is sending a message, or God's way of being anonymous. With this in mind, it is not surprising that some people look to synchronicity as a way of getting information, or insights, that may help in decision-making.

Synchronicity is related to luck in that both are often regarded as coming from 'out there', and that some people experience more 'meaningful connections' than others, in the same way that some have, or appear to have, more good luck than others. Perhaps it is a matter of being on the right wavelength, of being 'tuned in', in order to receive the signals. Gamblers, who are constantly looking around for signs and portents that may point the way to good luck, will make much of synchronicitous events and try to use them for their benefit. They will regard them as signals, or guidelines, to good luck, that the way is being pointed out to them and all they have to do is follow.

Serendipity
Serendipity refers to a situation or event in which something fortunate or desirable is discovered by accident or chance, when one is looking for something else. Serendip was the ancient Persian name for Ceylon, now Sri Lanka. Horace Walpole, the son of the first British Prime Minister, Sir Robert Walpole, used the word 'serendipity' in 1754 in a letter to Horace Mann. Walpole referred to what he called 'a silly fairy tale called *The Three Princes of Serendipity*', who, as they travelled, 'were always making discoveries, by accident or sagacity, of things which they were not in quest of'. The word 'sagacity' is significant here and reminds one of Pasteur's statement that 'chance favours the prepared mind'. The three princes were sagacious and therefore able to make connections or deductions from their observations that others would probably not have made, in reaching conclusions and decisions. Had the princes not been clever, observant and open-minded, it is unlikely that they would have made such discoveries 'by accident'.

Although scientists might scoff at such things as serendipity, luck, chance, or lucky chance (call them what you will), it is a fact that they have played a major role in discoveries in the sciences, particularly in the fields of chemistry, pharmacology, medicine and physics, as well as in the area of exploration.

'Name the greatest inventor of all,' asked Mark Twain, and the answer he gave was, 'Accident'. Franklin P Adams said, 'I find that a great part of the information I have was acquired by looking up something and finding something else on the way'. For American writer Lawrence Block, serendipity means to 'look for something, find something else, and realise that what you've found is more suited to your needs than what you thought you were looking for.' For the Dutch ophthalmologist Pek van Andel, 'Serendipity is the art of making an unsought finding'.

It was a serendipitous event – the fall of an apple (there is no evidence that it landed on his head) – that is to said to have started Newton thinking about gravity. Another example was that of Archimedes jumping from the tub, shouting 'Eureka', upon realising that the amount of water displaced by his body in the bathtub was the same as his volume, and that the same principle could be used to obtain the volume of irregular objects (like the crown he had been given in order to determine its gold content). These are well-known examples of serendipity, when 'something clicked' and things became clear, but there are dozens of other examples, particularly in the fields mentioned above. A few will be given here.

Chemistry
In 1953, Patsy Sherman was experimenting to find a rubber compound that could be used to withstand the effects of aircraft fuel. She accidentally spilt some of it on her tennis shoe and, when she tried to clean the shoe, she found the compound would not wash off. The idea came to her that this compound could be used to protect materials against spills. She had discovered what became Scotchgard˚ moisture repellent, which is now widely used for the protection of leather and fabrics.

When working as an assistant to Louis Pasteur, the French chemist Hilaire de Chardonnet accidentally spilt a bottle of collodion. When the liquid evaporated, he was able to pull away thin strands that held together. He had just discovered the first commercially-viable artificial silk, developed by others as rayon.

Alfred Nobel, the inventor of dynamite and well-known for the prizes that bear his name, came up with the explosive substance by accidentally mixing nitroglycerine and collodion (gun cotton).

During World War II, the American James Wright was trying to find a substitute for rubber and ended up with Silly Putty˚.

While trying to find a new refrigeration gas, Roy J Plunkett ended up instead with a slippery substance. Now known as Teflon˚, it was initially used for lubrication.

Carl Ludwig Reichenbach put creosote on wooden posts to discourage dogs from urinating on them. They continued to do so, however, and a dark blue appeared on the posts. It was called pittacal, the first commercially-produced synthetic dye.

The British chemist William Ramsay discovered helium while looking for argon.

No fewer than three artificial sweeteners were discovered by accident. In 1967, Karl Claus accidentally discovered Acesulfame. Michael Sveda inadvertently contaminated a compound he was working on by smoking a cigarette and the result was cyclamate. James Schlatter wanted to develop a chemical to test a drug being used for ulcers when he discovered Aspartame.

Medicine and biology
The English physician Edward Jenner noticed that milkmaids did not contract smallpox because they had been exposed to cowpox. This gave him the idea of vaccination.
Two Japanese virologists, Yasu-ichi Nagano and Yasuhiko Kajima, were trying to come up with a better vaccine for smallpox and discovered the antiviral, interferon.

Charles Robert Richet was using dogs to test their reaction to sea anemone toxin. Dogs which on the first occasion had shown no reaction to the toxin developed such reactions rapidly when used a second time. This phenomenon is now known as anaphylaxis.

Pharmacology
Nitrous oxide (better known as laughing gas) had been known for its ability to produce uncontrollable laughter, but it was not until Humphry Davy, a British chemist, tested it on himself and a few of his friends that its anaesthetic properties were discovered. Davy observed that the gas, as well as inducing laughter, greatly reduced the sensation of pain, even when the person was still semi-conscious.

Dr Carl Djerassi discovered the first oral contraceptive ('The Pill') when he accidentally produced synthetic progesterone, which was later altered to make it possible to be taken orally.

Retin-A, which is derived from Vitamin A, was initially used to treat acne. A side effect was soon noticed – it reduced facial wrinkles in some older users. Now it is used for its anti-wrinkle properties.

Minoxidil was first used to treat hypertension. It was soon observed that some bald patients who used the medicine began to grow new hair. Now minoxidil is used to treat baldness.

Before going on holiday, Alexander Fleming did not properly disinfect cultures of bacteria and, when he returned to the laboratory, he found that they had been contaminated by penicillium mould. He noted that the bacteria had been killed, and, as he had a lot of experience of antibacterial substances, he had the 'prepared mind' to understand the implications of the dead bacteria.

Albert Hoffman, a Swiss scientist, was cycling home one evening when he had the world's first 'acid trip'. In order to test its properties, he had earlier taken a small amount of a substance he had been working on and was now having this psychedelic experience. He had discovered LSD. This is what he had to say of his discovery: 'It is true that my discovery of LSD was a chance discovery, but it was the outcome of planned experiments and these experiments took place in the framework of systematic, pharmaceutical, chemical research. It could better be described as serendipity.'

Sildenafil citrate was first studied as a possible treatment for angina pectoris and hypertension. Early trials showed little promise as a heart medicine, but it was noted that it did have a rather interesting side effect – it was very good at inducing penile erection. Viagra' had arrived.

The drug l-dopa was used to treat Parkinson's disease. When it was administered to older patients in a sanatorium, it was noticed that some of them had rediscovered an interest in sex.

Astronomy and physics
The astronomer William Herschel was gazing into the heavens, looking for comets. He noticed what he thought was a comet but its circular orbit made him think again. He had discovered the planet Uranus. Herschel was particularly serendipitous because he also discovered infrared radiation while he was checking the temperatures of different colours of light. He had put the light through a prism and was measuring the temperatures of the different colours. When he measured beyond the red end of the spectrum, he was surprised to find that the temperature was higher, proving that there was invisible radiation outside the red end of the spectrum.

The French scientist Henri Becquerel hit upon radioactivity when using photographic plates to experiment on phosphorescent materials. In the process, he also discovered uranium.

While working with cathode ray tubes, Wilhelm Roentgen discovered X-rays when he noticed that, although his equipment had an opaque covering, some fluorescent papers that happened to be in the laboratory were lit up.

Johannes Georg Bednorz and Karl Alexander Muller won the 1987 Nobel Prize for Physics for their discovery of high-temperature superconductivity. They had been looking for a perfect electrical insulator.

Inventions
Ruth Wakefield wanted to make chocolate-drop biscuits, but she did not have any chocolate. She got a sweet bar, broke it into pieces and put them into the cake mix. The chocolate chip cookie was on its way.

In 1898, the Kellogg brothers had cooked some grain, but had neglected to check on it. A day later, when they tried to roll it over, they found it had become flaky. Today we call those flakes cornflakes.

An engineer working for Canon accidentally put a hot soldering iron near his pen and, a few moments later, the ink squirted from the pen. Ink jet printers are the result.

Charles Goodyear accidentally discovered the vulcanization of rubber when he put a piece of rubber that had been mixed with sulphur on a hot bit of metal.

A US engineer called Richard James accidentally knocked a spring off his bench and, after noticing its strange movements, invented the Slinky®.

Geographical discoveries
Leiv Eiriksson is regarded by many as the first European to discover America, in around 1000. He had landed in order to take shelter from a storm.

In 1492, Christopher Columbus accidentally rediscovered America while he was looking for a route to India and the Spice Islands.

Vicente Pinzon discovered South America when he turned up on the coast of Brazil while exploring the West Indies.

The foregoing is only a small sample of the large number of discoveries and inventions that came about with a big helping hand from serendipity or luck. Pek van Andel's other definition of serendipity comes to mind here: 'Serendipity is looking for a needle in a haystack and finding a farmer's daughter'. Even the most sceptical would find it hard to deny the reality of luck here, albeit pointing out the 'prepared mind' of the inventors, discoverer or explorer. As Isaac Asimov said, 'The most exciting phrase to hear in science is not "Eureka" but "That's funny…"'. It is a moment of inspiration, insight and clarity, when things come together and one feels in tune with the universe.

Unfortunately, there is always the other side of the coin. Not all chance happenings are good, or desirable or lucky. Being in the wrong place at the wrong time, becoming a 'collateral damage' statistic or the victim of an unlikely accident, would be examples of what William Boyd called zemblanity, the opposite of serendipity. If serendipity is 'the lucky chance of finding something we did not know we were looking for', as Glauco Ortalano said, then zemblanity is accidentally finding something we definitely were not looking for. Looking for a needle in a haystack and finding neither a needle nor a farmer's daughter but a thorn, rat or snake instead, could be classified as zemblanity.

But, it is best to be positive and, possibly, attract some good luck. Look at it this way. Astronomers tell us that man is composed mainly of carbon, oxygen and hydrogen, materials that came from the Sun and stars. We are made from stardust! How serendipitous is that?

Collective Unconscious

Freud wrote that the mind is divided into the conscious and the unconscious. The conscious mind is the part of which we are most aware. Memories, thoughts and feelings are stored there. These things are closely related to the ego, the 'I', the things that make 'I' me, a unique individual. The ego relates to what a person thinks and feels they are. There may be certain things that the conscious mind does not like to dwell on, such as traumatic experiences, unhappy memories or shameful deeds. These are pushed, or 'suppressed', according to Freud, into the subconscious mind where, we hope, they will stay put and not rise up to cause us problems.

Carl Jung was a disciple of Freud, but the two men disagreed and parted ways. Freud wrote of the personal unconscious mind, but Jung added to this what he called the collective unconscious. This he regarded as a kind of universal unconscious. He said that it goes right back to the earliest days of mankind and holds mythological and religious symbols, which he called 'archetypes', and were the background to our thought processes. These archetypes were, he believed, patterns that were common to all mankind and, as a result, some have called it the 'universal mind', though this is not exactly Jung's meaning. The idea of such a prototype was not new. Plato, the Stoics and St Augustine wrote of a type of perfect spiritual reality which came before physical realities.

It is tempting to take the idea of the collective unconscious out of the field of psychiatry and look at it from a spiritual, occult or aesthetic viewpoint. Some contend that the collective unconscious contains not just the past, but also the present and future, and the person's ability to 'tap into' this will determine their luck and quality of life. This tapping in does not necessarily have to be a conscious act, or even an act of will, but rather the work of the unconscious mind itself. This leads to the belief that a person could reach into this domain in their dreams, in a trance or in some other 'heightened' state, and those who are sensitive to the messages or guidance received in this way will have better luck and be in a stronger position to chart a way through life.

Akashic record

The word *akasha* comes from Sanskrit and can be translated as 'space' or 'ether'. It refers to a large collection of mystical knowledge which is said to be stored in a type of giant library or computer bank in a non-physical domain. Some even refer to it as 'the mind of God'.

The Akashic records are believed by devotees to contain records of the entire cosmos, as well as all of human knowledge and experience. Some even claim that they hold the records of all animals, plants and minerals. These records, it is said, can be accessed by prayer, yoga, astral travel, drugs, fasting, meditation or visualisation. They are said to have been accumulating since the beginning of time. Some contend that early man had the ability to access these records and, in more modern times, Edgar Cayce, Helena Petrovna Blatavasky and Rudolf Steiner, among others, claimed to be able to read them. In Steiner's case, Adolf Hitler (whom some claim was also able to reach into the records and was known to have had an interest in such exotica) wanted him killed because of his supposed knowledge of the Akashic records. However, Steiner's friends got to know of this, and even when and where the planned attack was to take place, and managed to save him.

Edgar Cayce, whose strange powers many accept as genuine and who could be considered a force for good on the planet, was, according to Dr Wesley H Ketchum, 'in direct communication with all other subconscious minds'. Were this so, it would explain the vast knowledge Cayce possessed, knowledge which one would not have expected him to possess, in fields which he had not studied.

The Akashic record is similar, in some ways, to Jung's collective unconscious. If such exists, and if there are people who can access and utilise the information that is said to be stored there, then, in a deterministic universe, they would have the ability to predict the future (in a limited way), as the future is merely a cause/effect extension of the past and present. Many clairvoyants (also known as sensitives) and fortune-tellers would no doubt claim such abilities. While such an ability may not enable one to predict next week's winning lottery numbers, or which horse will come in first in the Kentucky Derby, any knowledge of the future that could be used to make better decisions in the present would be valuable. The mind of man is restless and inquisitive. For many, knowledge of the past and present is not enough – they want to know the future as well. People who had such knowledge of the future, either consciously or unconsciously, and however limited the information, would be more likely to make good decisions, have better lives and be regarded as lucky.

Many people who consult fortune-tellers, contact psychic hotlines or read their daily horoscopes may treat, or pretend to treat, such matters as 'a bit of fun'. But, deep down, there must be something more, a desire to get a sneak preview of the future, or maybe some information or advice that would help them to prosper and be lucky. Otherwise, why bother with fortune-tellers, psychics and horoscopes? Perhaps they are like Hamlet when he says to his friend, Horatio, 'There are more things in Heaven and Earth, Horatio, than are dreamt of in your philosophy'. Maybe, after all, there is something to fortune-telling and other such exotica that the cynic, sceptic and scientists are missing out on? Or maybe not!

As far as we know, we are the only intelligent life form in the universe. Intelligence is a fine thing, but it is a double-edged sword. It can solve the most abstract problems, but it can also keep you awake at three in the morning, worrying about mortgage payments or that small lump in your neck, matters over which a less intelligent sheep or cockroach would be unlikely to lose sleep. Because of man's intelligence and ability to look to the past and the future, rather than living in an eternal present like the other creatures with which he shares this planet, there are times when he feels not just alone but lonely. Despite his intelligence, there are numerous things which he cannot understand, explain or control. All around there is suffering and hatred, as well as mercy and love, violence and death, and kindness and birth. It can become confusing, even bewildering. Is it any wonder that he will, occasionally, try to look outside the known, to speculate, hope or seek assistance? Some will talk to God, others to themselves – one will talk to a psychiatrist, another to a good listener or a friend. Still others will look for guidance in how tossed bones fall on the ground, the pattern of tea-leaves in the bottom of a cup or the lines on their hands. When logic and common sense do not provide satisfactory answers, it is to be expected that some will look for answers where logic and common sense do not seem to play a part.

We can blame it all on Pandora. Had she done what she was told and not opened the box, we would not be in this mess. But, oh no, she just had to find out what was inside! Well, it could be worse. At least we were left with Hope.

In fact, we should count ourselves lucky to be here at all. Geneticists tell us that modern Homo sapiens has very little genetic variety. It was not always so. At some point in the distant past, possibly about 70,000 years ago, the human race seems to have gone through a kind of 'bottleneck', and only a small number made it through. According to the Toba catastrophe theory, the total human population may have been as little as 10,000 people, all of whom were genetically very similar. A massive super-eruption at Toba in Sumatra, Indonesia, sometime between 69,000 and 77,000 years ago, is thought by many to have been the cause. The theory postulates that the huge eruption was followed by ten years of 'volcanic winter' and a few hundred more years of cooling. Today, the caldera is the giant Lake Toba. The volcano is likely to erupt again in the future, like the super-volcano under Yellowstone National Park, with catastrophic consequences. The fact that there was so little genetic variation in Homo sapiens after the near-extinction event would suggest that those who survived came from a particular area and group. Of course, extinctions have been very common through geological time and continue to occur. The main difference now is that we are around to help out. According to Edward O Wilson of Harvard University in his 2002 book, *The Future of Life*, at current rates of human destruction of the biosphere, one-half of all species will be extinct in 100 years. In *The Pattern of Evolution*, Niles Eldredge states, 'It is ... well established that the earth is currently undergoing yet another mass extinction event ... and it is clear that the major agent for this event is Homo sapiens'.

Taken all in all, we (if not many other species) are lucky we are here, a matter of random chance. One is reminded of the quip by W C Fields – 'Aw, life. It's a strange business. A man is lucky if he gets out of it alive.'

Chapter 7

Luck and Related Phenomena

The only sure thing about luck is that it will change.
Wilson Mizner

It's hard to detect good luck – it looks so much like something you've earned.
Frank A Clark

Luck is a dividend of sweat. The more you sweat, the luckier you get.
Ray Kroc

Those who have succeeded in anything and don't mention luck are kidding themselves.
Larry King

We will either find a way or make one.
Hannibal of Carthage

God provides food for the birds, but He does not take it to their nests.
Irish saying

Astrology

As stated earlier, man has a great curiosity about the future and tries many ways to find out what may be in store for him. Astrology is one such way. Whether one regards astrology as a science, pseudo-science, proto-science, art or superstition, the fact is that, like luck, there are hundreds of millions of people all over the world who have an interest, or belief, in it.

After studying the positions and movement of celestial bodies, astrologers draw up horoscopes, claiming that the movements in the heavens are mirrored in, or influence, events on Earth. Astrology has been around for at least 2,000 years, and probably longer. In that time, many separate traditions have developed and it has become a vast and complex field. The Babylonians, Arabs, Persians, Egyptians, Greeks, Chinese, Indians and Mayas all developed their own unique brands.

Horoscopes were, and are, traditionally drawn up for significant times in life. Many consider the time of a person's birth the most significant and the branch of astrology that specialises in this is called natal astrology. Once the exact moment of a person's birth is known, the astrologer can draw up a diagram of the heavens and use this to determine the significance of the alignments and positions of various celestial bodies at that moment. The heavenly bodies were, and are, believed to have a significant effect on people. People born at a certain time would be deemed lucky, while those born at another time would be regarded as being likely to have a lot of bad luck in their lives.

Katarchic or electional astrology uses a horoscope to advise on the best time to begin a new venture or for an individual to take a significant step in life, such as getting married or deciding to relocate.

For those who have a specific question, there is horary astrology. The astrologer will consult a chart for the time in question in an attempt to answer the question. Taking a broader view, there is mundane (world) astrology, which deals with issues like natural disasters and important events in politics and religion.

In all cases, the celestial bodies are believed to have an influence on Earth, its inhabitants and its events. For those who believe that luck is something that comes from 'out there', it would be natural to take an interest in astrology and try to find out how things are 'out there' in relation to their own lives.

Those who regard astrology as a pseudo-science or, worse, superstition, must nevertheless give it credit for the contribution it has made to astronomy. Beginning around the time of the Renaissance and the introduction of scientific method to the study of the world and the heavens, astronomy developed, slowly and gradually, from astrology and became a science. Astrology continued on its separate path and was not subject to the rigours of science.

Astrology was not always held in such low esteem or regarded as negatively as it is today. Pythagoras, Plato, Copernicus, Tycho Brae, Galileo, Kepler and Newton, among others, had great interest in astrology and found it worthy of study. When one of his friends castigated Isaac Newton for his interest in astrology, the great scientist is said to have snapped, 'I understand, Sir. You don't.'

Astrology has also contributed to language. The word 'influenza' is related to the word 'influence', as certain illnesses, particularly at certain times of the year, were thought to be caused by the malignant influence of heavenly bodies. 'Disaster' comes from the Latin for 'star', and 'lunatics' were so called because it was thought that the moon (Luna) influenced their insanity. 'Venereal' is from Venus, the Roman goddess of love, and 'martial' is from Mars, the god of war.

Despite this, most scientists now regard astrology as a pseudo-science or superstition. They say that it has no scientific basis and cannot be verified by experimentation or observation. However, some astrologers are conducting research and attempting to put their discipline on a scientific footing, while others claim that the scientific method is not appropriate to their field.

There has been one notable exception to this scientific scepticism. Michel Gauquelin, a French statistician and psychologist, while highly sceptical about the claims of astrology, believed he had detected a connection between certain positions of the planets at the time of birth and particular human traits. His studies seemed to indicate that people born when Mars was in a particular part of the heavens had greater athletic ability. However, this 'Mars effect' has not gained respectability or general acceptance among the scientific community.

In a way, astrology and luck occupy the same type of limbo existence – believed in by hundreds of millions, but getting no scientific recognition. Most scientists would consider them beneath their interest and not worthy of study. Indeed, were they to express an interest in these matters it might affect their credibility and professional standing. This is rather unscientific, as science prides itself on being open-minded and not rushing to accept, or reject, without exhaustive proof.

In the case of luck, the situation is probably more nebulous, as there is nothing tangible to point to, and nothing to weigh, measure or dissect. With astrology, at least there are the planets, stars and celestial movements, which can be seen. Luck is likely to remain in the wilderness unless some scientist can catch some, take it to his laboratory, measure it, weight it, probe it, subject it to electrical charges, test its reaction with various chemicals and subject it to every conceivable test. Then he might be able to come up with some kind of theory, hypothesis or statistical analysis. These would then need to be tested and proved by thousands of further tests and experiments. At the end of all of this, there might be something definite, or there might not. But, no matter what science might prove, seem to prove or disprove, about luck or astrology, it is likely that there would be many who would still adhere to their original beliefs.

Fortune-telling

Fortune-telling is an umbrella term for a host of activities that predict, attempt to predict, or claim to predict a person's future. It has worldwide acceptance and uses many different techniques.

In America and Europe, despite an increase in scepticism and cynicism, and various prohibitions by church and state, fortune-telling is still widely practised. As many people are curious about their futures and what luck has in store for them, no matter how strict the prohibitions against it, it is unlikely that fortune-telling could be stamped out.

Among the methods used in the west to predict the future are cartomancy (using cards), tasseography (reading the tea-leaves in a cup), crystallography (using a crystal ball), and palm-reading. Other fortune-tellers claim to get their information from spirits or disembodied entities and pass this on to their clients. They have no need for any paraphernalia.

The areas of life which concern most people when it comes to fortune telling are love, finances, career, health and family, and it is generally in those areas that fortune-tellers operate most frequently. Such questions as 'Will I meet the love of my life?', 'Will I win the lottery or come into a fortune?', Will I get a good job?' and 'How long will I live?' would be typical enough questions. No one can blame people for wanting to know about those things in advance, for trying to find a way through lives that can be lonely, difficult or fraught with what is perceived as ill fortune. The question is whether such things are knowable in advance. Based on information obtained from fortune-tellers and psychics (sensitives) and psychic hotline advertisements, it would appear that more women than men consult fortune-tellers and that they are, not surprisingly, more likely to be consulted at significant (now known as 'passage') times in people's lives, such as before getting married, changing jobs or making a major financial decision.

While fortune-tellers will generally not reveal the names of their clients (and most practitioners are bound by some kind of code of ethics), there have been statements by some well-known fortune-tellers that they have been consulted by politicians, Hollywood actors and actresses, company managers and high-powered financial consultants The reaction to such news is usually mixed – either horror that such people could be so gullible, alarm that major decisions are left in the hands of sensitives, or confirmation that fortune-telling is a genuine science, or art, that is used even by the rich, famous and powerful.

The official reaction to fortune-telling is also mixed. In the west, fortune-telling for remuneration (money or some other form of payment) is illegal in certain jurisdictions and legal in others. Some districts require that fortune-tellers (more often referred to in these circumstances as 'psychic consultants' or 'spiritual advisers') possess a licence or are bonded. On the other hand, if the fortune-telling is carried out for entertainment and no remuneration is obtained, there is no legal difficulty. From a practical point of view, any sensible lawmaker will realise that some people will continue to consult fortune-tellers even if this is made illegal, and it would seem foolhardy to criminalise such behaviour. It would probably turn out like Prohibition, a law that was widely ignored and broken, and was eventually repealed. The practice would likely go 'underground' if banned, and become more secretive. However, lawmakers have the duty to protect the public, and they have to ensure that people are safeguarded from unscrupulous or dishonest practitioners, who would cheat or deceive them. The major difficulty is that there is no recognised diploma, degree or other official qualification that can be obtained in the field that would prove that a person had undergone a course of study and achieved knowledge and expertise up to a certain standard. Neither is there any recognised body that oversees or regulates the training, testing or supervision of fortune-tellers. The problem is one of 'quality control' and certification so that, in effect, there is nothing to stop anyone who is not a convicted criminal setting themselves up in business. In such a context, it is likely that there will be fraud and hoaxes, which does nothing to improve the image of fortune-telling among its practitioners, clients or the public at large.

Were one to consult a doctor, psychiatrist or other professional, one can do so in the knowledge that the person has some recognised qualification, is part of some professional organisation and can be subjected to sanction if they behave unprofessionally. Some fortune-tellers will counter that their area is not one that can be taught or learned, that it is a gift, that it is further enhanced by experience and that there is no need for an umbrella organisation. They will further point out that certain standards are adhered to, that client confidentiality is respected, and that the client's welfare is paramount.

In Asia, fortune-tellers are generally held in high esteem and are often respected and valued members of the community. It is not unusual for a businessman to seek advice from a fortune-teller, nor would he be ashamed to admit it. He would also feel relaxed discussing personal problems and seeking advice from one when his occidental counterpart would, more likely, be lying on a psychiatrist's couch. While seeking business or financial advice from someone who is not an 'expert' or has no qualification or experience in the field would be frowned on in the west, it is interesting to note that the most recent financial crisis started in the west and was not predicted or foreseen by most of those 'experts'. Many of those so-called 'experts' give contradictory advice and the ethical behaviour of some bankers and financial managers was worse than that of many who would be labelled fraudsters or hoaxers (such as fortune-tellers). Of course, these 'experts' will point out that financial cycles can be unpredictable and claim 'best endeavours'. If bankers and financiers can claim 'best endeavours', then surely others can too.

While there is great variety and complexity in oriental fortune-telling, with China, Taiwan, Japan and Korea following paths that diverge at many points, the general basis for fortune-telling in these countries is the belief in the five main compartments of life – fate, luck, feng shui, karma and education. This division goes back to a quotation that is attributed, by most schools, to Su Shi, who lived during the Song dynasty. In order to have a lucky and balanced life it was necessary to have these five elements in the correct proportions.

There is much disagreement as to the relative importance of these or the order in which they should be put. Some interpret them as indicating that one's fate is decided by luck, while others note that education can help one determine one's fate or luck. To complicate matters, some argue that a person's level of education is decided by their fate or that education on its own is of little use without luck.

Oriental fortune-tellers use a number of different methods in their attempts to delve into the future. One technique is reading the facial features, such as the eyes, nose and mouth, and using these to make predictions. The face is drawn and then divided into three sections – the upper, middle and lower. The upper section of the face was believed to tell one's future when young, the middle section predicted luck in middle age and the lower part dealt with old age. Reading of the palm is also used, as in the West. Fortune-tellers also use incense sticks, popularly known as Chi Chi sticks. The sticks, on which Chinese characters have been written, are put into a container which is then shaken until one falls out. The character on that stick is then interpreted.

In Africa, a wide variety of methods were, and are, used to predict the future. The best known is the procedure of 'throwing the bones'. In some cases, depending on the locality, stones, shells or other items may be used instead of bones. The bones (or other items) are usually marked and the fortune-teller or witchdoctor bases his reading on the positions of the bones and whether or not they touch. Other methods involve the use of eggs or water, but the aim is the same – to predict the future and to give information or advice to the person seeking it. Many of these fortune-tellers or witchdoctors may also double as herbalists and will usually be able to give 'medicine' to divert bad luck or attract good luck. As in the east, African fortune-tellers are usually highly respected, though this respect is often accompanied by a measure of fear or awe, as it is generally thought that they are in touch with spirits or 'higher powers' and it would do a person's luck no good at all were they to antagonise or upset them.

There are countless anecdotal accounts of apparently amazing predictions cited by fortune-tellers as proof of the efficacy of their trade. Believers accept these without question and use them as justification of their belief in fortune-telling. Sceptics look for other explanations for those alleged successes. Some will say that they appear to work because the person consulting the fortune teller believes in such practices and points to their state of mind rather than the competence of the fortune teller. The sceptics will also point out that some outcomes could be regarded as self-fulfilling prophesies that have been brought about by the believer altering his or her actions to fall in with the prediction. Believers will also be accused of confirmation bias – of talking about what is seen as a correct prediction while ignoring all the others that were not accurate.

Fortune-tellers are often accused of, or credited with, being experts at reading body language and other non-verbal communication, and at telling people what they want to hear. The fact that many predictions are couched in vague, ambiguous or general language means that such non-specific information could be given to a number of people with an equal probability of success. Examples of this might be, 'You have recently had some bad news' (many people have), 'You are having difficulty making a decision' (who hasn't?), or 'You are about to cross water' (there are a lot of water mains about). And, who is going to disagree if they are told, 'You have a beautiful aura', 'You are undervalued' or 'You have a generous spirit'? Often these sterling qualities will be regarded as earning good luck in the future. It would seem churlish to disagree.

If astrologers are right, then our destinies are written in the stars, from the moment of our birth. On the other hand, maybe Shakespeare had it right in *Julius Caesar*: 'The fault, dear Brutus, lies not in our stars, but in ourselves'. In *The Iliad*, when Homer asks, 'And which of the gods was it, I wonder, that put them up to fight?' he is assuming that men are acting on the prompting, and under the control, of the gods – in the lap of the gods. It is up to each individual to make up his mind on such matters. Are fortune-tellers (a) devious, manipulative, greedy fraudsters who prey on the naïve and the weak; (b) talented and/or gifted people who have special powers to see into the future and provide valuable guidance on the difficult journey through life; (c) something in between; or (d) none of the above?

Premonitions

From the Latin *praemonere* (to forewarn), a premonition is a warning, or feeling, that something, often unpleasant, is about to happen. Some may attribute this power to God or some other supernatural power, but it is well to look at some other possible explanations. The main point is to distinguish between a premonition – the 'feeling' that something is going to happen – and the possibility that it is based on evidence or a shrewd guess. Also, how probable or improbable is the thing you feel is about to happen? If there are dark clouds rolling in and someone says 'It's going to rain', you would hardly regard this as a premonition. It would be a rational prediction, based on the observed evidence, as the coming of rain from dark clouds is a frequent occurrence. Meteorologists do not claim to have premonitions about bad weather but will base their forecasts on the best available information from satellites and other sources.

When one looks at the evidence in support of premonitions, as provided by famous predictions, one would be inclined to decide that it is, at best, inconclusive. Nostradamus is said to have predicted, among many other things, the time of his death and even the date on which someone would open his tomb. But many of Nostradamus' predictions (or premonitions, as they were made long before they were meant to happen and could not have been based on information available to him at the time) are couched in very vague and ambiguous language (like that of some fortune-tellers or the oracles of old) and are open to any number of interpretations. Samuel Langhorne Clemens, better known as Mark Twain, was born when Halley's Comet was visible, and he predicted that he would die when the comet came around again. Halley's Comet reappeared on 18 May 1910, and Twain died one day later. Calpurnia, Julius Caesar's wife, is said to have had a dream on the night before his assassination that he would be killed. She told Julius but he went ahead with his plans and met his fate. Caesar was very unpopular among certain powerful sections of Roman society, as they believed that he wanted to be king (and the Romans had suffered enough with kings), and it was a strong possibility that someone would try to get him out of the way. Maybe Calpurnia knew this and it had preyed on her mind, resulting in the dream. Alternatively, it could have been something she ate.

Before his death in 1898, Otto Von Bismarck, the German statesman, is said to have predicted World War I. Bismarck was an accomplished and well-informed politician and diplomat, with an extensive knowledge of European affairs. Indeed, he had participated in and shaped many of them. In view of this, Bismarck's statement could be regarded as being a sound prediction based on knowledge rather than a premonition. It was more than just a 'feeling' or an impression. Abraham Lincoln is said to have had a premonition of his assassination. He dreamt that there were mourners gathered in the east wing of the White House. When he asked whom they were mourning he was told, 'The President'.

Another difficulty is that many premonitions seem to relate to rather minor events, such as 'I had a premonition that I was going to have an accident', or 'I just knew that the news would not be good'. While such events are interesting and provide a topic for conversation, they are hardly of cosmic importance or proof that one has seen into the future. At other times it may be an ominous feeling that something terrible is about to happen to you. Maybe such feelings, or premonitions, are the result of fear, apprehension, negativity or depression, rather than insight into the future. It is a matter on which conclusive answers are unlikely to be forthcoming.

While not denying that premonitions are possible – or even statistically probable, given all the people who live and have lived on the planet, the long period of time involved and the huge number of events that have occurred in that time – it is not easy to find definite proof of them. One of the difficulties is that the premonitions are often first revealed after the events have occurred, such as 'I had a premonition that was going to happen', and therefore must be suspect. There have been a number of predictions, based on premonitions, in the last 150 years, that the world was about to end. As far as we know, none of them has come true, though the point has been argued. One cult leader had predicted the end of the world but the date passed and the Earth still went on its way. There were disappointed and surprised acolytes and a leader who should have been embarrassed, even ashamed. But the man in question was ready for this, too. Displaying talents that would have made him an invaluable asset as a spin-doctor or political adviser had he not heard the call of religion, he pointed out, when questioned by the media, that the world had in fact ended. The 'elect' had been spirited away, presumably to a better place. It was just the unfortunate, unenlightened, unelected who were left behind that were so deluded that they could not see or comprehend what had happened. That sounded about right, for how could the ignorant, unelected be expected to understand such matters? There was one problem, however. If the world had ended, then why was our cult leader still about and not in a better place with the elected? Could it be that he had been found unworthy?

Premonitions are related to predicting, and there are times when the line between can become fuzzy. Scientists are getting better at foretelling certain outcomes, but these are usually referred to as predictions or probabilities. The use of surveys, statistics and exit polls have made the prediction of election results close to an exact science in some cases, with even the degree of possible error being known. But in many of these cases the degree of complexity, or the number of variables and possible outcomes, may not be too great. Predicting whether the Democrat or Republican candidate will win a US presidential election is something like picking the winner in a two-horse race. Now, were someone to predict that Mr or Ms X, who has not yet been born, will be elected US president sometime towards the end of the 21st century, then that would be worth looking out for.

While not as common in reality as some would like, premonitions are common and popular in novels and movies. There is no shortage of fictional characters that have premonitions and are not slow to spread them about, but being able to write one's own future in a work of fiction is a big asset when it comes to premonitions.

One could credit some of the Old Testament prophets, many of whom told of coming doom and gloom, as having had premonitions. They believed that their prophetic knowledge came from God. They regarded themselves as merely conduits, lines of communication between God and man. Perhaps some modern fortune-tellers, or sensitives, can tap into powers that others cannot comprehend.

Telling people that you have had a premonition is not always a good thing. Either the bad thing you anticipated happens or you may end up with egg on your face, which sounds like a lose/lose situation. It is best to bear in mind the words of the American sportsman, Yogi Berra: 'It is very hard to predict, especially when you are talking about the future'.

Precognition

Precognition is the foreknowledge of events or having knowledge of a place or person through extraordinary perception. J W Dunne carried out the first study of precognition in 1927. In his book *An Experiment with Time*, Dunne described his precognitive dreams, in which future events were made known to him. Some of the events were of a trivial or personal nature, but many were of the kind that made the headlines the following day. Dunne was quite worried at first by these dreams, but was reassured when he learned that such precognitive dreams were quite common.

Forty years after the publication of Dunne's book, the British Premonition Bureau was set up by J A Barker, a London psychiatrist, in the hope of getting some advance warning of disasters. Barker did find some individuals who could tell of calamities yet to come but, unfortunately, they were unable to be specific about the times.

If precognition is a valid phenomenon, the question is whether those who possess that ability are lucky or unlucky, blessed or cursed. Knowing that something bad is going to happen to you, a friend or indeed to an area (such as an earthquake or volcanic eruption) but being unable to do anything to prevent it, is hardly the type of information most people would want. But maybe they could do something to prevent things from happening. That would give rise to a difficulty. If a person knows of an upcoming event through precognition and then prevents it from happening, then the event never happened and could not have been foreseen.

This is a bit like the case of Cassandra, the daughter of King Priam of Troy and Queen Hecuba. Apollo was smitten by her and gave her the gift of prophecy. However, when Cassandra spurned his affection, he retaliated by putting a curse on her – her prophecies would not be heeded. The 'gift' of prophecy was to bring her nothing but grief and torment. When the Greeks rolled the Wooden Horse up to the walls of Troy, Cassandra warned the people of the danger, but no one listened to her. She foretold her own death and that of Agamemnon. When Troy fell, Cassandra was taken back to Mycenae by Agamemnon as a spoil of war. His wife, Clytemnestra, and her boyfriend, Aegisthus, murdered both Agamemnon and Cassandra. She had foreseen all this but was powerless to prevent it.

Intuition

Intuition is the ability, or apparent ability, of certain people to obtain information so rapidly that reasoning does not seem to be involved. It is like the 'gut feeling' that is often not given much weight or respect. To know something 'intuitively' means that you have not reached that knowledge by reasoning or logic, you 'just know', and may not be able to explain why. Sometimes this is referred to as a 'sixth sense'.

Intuition has traditionally been treated with more respect by scientists than premonitions. They have even gone so far as to give the name Intuition Peak to a high point on the South Shetland Islands in the Antarctic, in recognition of what intuition has contributed to science.

A doctor who has been treating patients for years may 'know' what a person is suffering from without an examination. Of course, years of experience have enabled him to read signals or some other symptoms of an illness very soon after seeing some patients. This intuition will be proved right or wrong by examination of the patient, but it will often be right. In the same way, an experienced detective might 'just know' that a person is guilty, even before questioning that person or having access to any other proof of guilt. However, doctors, detectives and others have to be careful not to rely on intuition alone, as it may not always be right.

People who are considered highly intuitive have been noticed to be adept at picking up on non-verbal and other signals. The role played by experience is significant, but not complete. As mentioned earlier, the human brain is very good at creating and recognising patterns, so perhaps much of intuition is the rapid calling-up of these established patterns.

Jung divided 'psychological types' into four categories. In his diagrammatical representation, he placed intuition and sensation on opposite ends of one axis, while feeling and thinking were placed on the other axis. Jung postulated that one of those Ego functions would be dominant, or more developed, than the others, while the one on the same axis, but opposed to it, would be weakest. So, if intuition was dominant, sensation would be least developed. Because of this, experts in particular fields will be able to make rapid, apparently intuitive, decisions as the brain patterns in their particular field will be well established. After this initial intuitive flash, and more slowly if time permits, there will be a careful analysis of the factors that have led to this conclusion. But, when a very quick decision is required, intuition alone is often at work.

It is easy to see how others could regard people who can make quick, intuitive decision as being lucky or gifted. Expressions such as 'Lucky beggar, he always seems to do the right thing' may be a tribute to intuition rather than luck. But then, people who have this talent can indeed be considered lucky. In normal circumstances, this type of circular argument (he is lucky because he is intuitive and intuitive because he is lucky) does not usually get one very far. A chicken-and-egg type impasse may be reached. Despite this, the fund manager who always seems to make the right investment and the actor who repeatedly chooses the right parts will sometimes be called lucky rather than intuitive.

When it comes to games of chance, relying on intuition may be very dangerous. Being successful at games such as roulette or lotteries is not, by its very nature, the type of activity that can be improved or honed by experience or practice. Just because a person had been playing roulette or buying lottery tickets for years does not mean that they are 'experienced' players who are more likely to win than others who have been doing so for a shorter time. There have been cases where winners have sensed winning numbers, but this is not something that is easy to quantify and should not be relied upon too much. It is much easier to be intuitive (and right) about something that has a high degree of probability than situations where the outcome is purely random.

There are also things in life that are counter-intuitive, where one's intuition tells one a particular thing but this turns out to be incorrect. There are various ways of interpreting data or situations and a person cannot always be certain of drawing the right conclusions. To make matters worse, intuition can often be very subjective. In this context, it is well to keep in mind the case of Russell's chicken. Bertrand Russell told the story of a chicken that was living on a farm. Every morning, the farmer brought it food and water. From this the chicken concluded (possibly even intuited) that the farmer liked it very much. After a while, the chicken noticed that the amounts of food and water seemed to be increasing. From this, it concluded that the farmer's liking for it had increased. Then, one morning, the farmer turned up with a large knife.

Superstition

A superstition is a belief, or practice, that is regarded as irrational or unreasonable, usually relating to magic, luck or the supernatural. That would be the definition of someone who was not superstitious. Those who are superstitious would not agree that their beliefs or behaviour were irrational or unreasonable. The word is usually used in a pejorative manner.

Man has been superstitious since early times and most primitive societies were controlled by a set of beliefs and observances, many of which would have made little sense if subjected to logical thinking. In later times, the Catholic Church often branded as superstitious practices with which they disagreed (apart from those that were regarded as heretical or schismatic). After the Reformation, the tables were turned somewhat, with reformers branding as superstitious certain Catholic practices such as the use of incense and rosary beads.

Superstitions vary from culture to culture, but usually they are associated with the dead, cemeteries, animals, gambling, luck and death. As with some other areas relating to magic or irrational belief, superstitions can be regarded as a faulty interpretation of cause and effect. Because one thing happens after another, the false assumption is made that the second event was the result of, or otherwise connected to, the first. So, if a person walked under a ladder and a short time later something bad or undesirable happened which was considered bad luck, he would associate this bad luck with walking under the ladder. (It is of interest to note that walking under a ladder is considered unlucky, rather than dangerous.) In the case where a superstitious person breaks a mirror, has a black cat cross his path or some other such 'unlucky' event occurs, and something bad subsequently happens, this will reinforce his belief. On the other hand, if there is a broken mirror or black cat incident and nothing bad happens, this will not change the person's belief. Their thinking is that the absence of something undesirable happening on this occasion does not mean that it will not happen on the next. They will persist in their belief, or behaviour, 'just in case…'. Were the person asked to explain how the ladder, mirror or cat brought bad luck, they would likely be at a loss to account for the connection.

There are hundreds of superstitions all over the world, varying between cultures. Even the most sophisticated societies and individuals can be superstitious. In the theatre, it is considered bad luck to mention the name of Shakespeare's tragedy, *Macbeth*. It is more usually referred to as 'the Scottish play'. The words 'good luck' should never be used in the theatre, the phrase 'break a leg' being preferred. Because some of the patterns on the tail feathers of a peacock look like an eye, some performers regard it as 'the evil eye' and peacocks are not welcome. Sailors are also traditionally superstitious. Whistling on board a ship is considered bad luck as it is believed to bring on an unfavourable wind. Saying the word 'pig' or sticking a knife in the deck are not advised. As both acting and seafaring are professions in which luck is regarded as playing a large part – as both audiences and the sea can be unpredictable and cruel – it is as advisable to take every precaution.

If you blow out all the candles on your birthday cake with one breath, it is a good sign and your unspoken wish will come true. Breaking a mirror is said to bring seven years of bad luck as the mirror was seen as the image of the soul, and a broken soul took time to heal. Many people in the west regard the number 13 as unlucky and some hotels will not put that number on a floor level, using instead 12A or jumping from 12 to 14. (In China, Korea and Japan, on the other hand, 13 is not considered unlucky, but the number 4 is, as the sound of the word resembles that of the word for 'death'.) Friday the 13th is considered particularly unlucky, though a check through history for unlucky or disastrous events that happened on that day and date would not bear this out. It is considered unlucky to whistle or sleep at table and if the palm of your right hand is itchy, it means that you are going to receive money. If you drop a fork, a woman will visit; a dropped knife means a male visitor and a dropped spoon means a child will visit.

Certain people, such as gravediggers and swineherds, are or were considered unlucky, while chimney sweeps are said to be lucky. Some people were thought to have the 'evil eye' or 'hot eye' and it was definitely bad luck to be around them. The Austrian physicist Wolfgang Pauli was said to have had a disastrous effect on scientific equipment when he was present in the laboratory. His friend and fellow scientist, Otto Stern, would not even allow Pauli to enter his Hamburg laboratory, so notorious was the 'Pauli effect', as it became known. Pauli did not even need to be present to cause havoc. While an experiment was being conducted at the University of Göttingen, a piece of equipment stopped working. As Pauli was not present in the laboratory, it seemed he could not be blamed on this occasion. However, it turned out that he was at Göttingen railway station at the time, en route from Copenhagen to Zurich. As well as being a theoretical scientist (being an experimental scientist would seem to be out of the question) Pauli was also interested in the paranormal and it is known that he believed in the 'Pauli effect'.

Magpies can be lucky or unlucky, depending on their number, as the following rhyme shows:

One for sorrow, two for joy,
Three to get married, four to die.
Five for silver, six for gold
Seven for a secret never to be told.

A black cat crossing one's path is regarded as lucky in some cultures and unlucky in others. Putting shoes on a bed or table is considered unlucky by many, as is the presence of a frog or robin inside the house. A cricket in the house, however, is considered lucky.

As we have seen, actors and sailors are, or at least were, superstitious, but gamblers would probably be considered the most superstitious. As with acting and seafaring, gambling is an activity in which the unknown, or unexpected, can play a significant part. Many gamblers carry a rabbit's foot, four-leaf clover or some other 'lucky' items which, they believe, will bring them good fortune. Some gamblers engage in ritualised behaviour which they feel will help them to win. Some sportsmen are known to have what they consider 'lucky' garments or footwear.

If a person believes that certain objects, or behaviour, will help them to be successful, there would be no point in trying to convince them otherwise. As a person's mental state has a great influence on their actions, it is possible that gamblers, sportsmen or others who have their 'lucky' items or have performed their 'lucky' ritual before taking part in their chosen activity will feel not just luckier, but more positive and confident. While it is easy to see how this could affect a sportsman's performance, it is less easy to see how it could help a gambler, particularly one who is engaging in a gamble in which there is a high degree of randomness.

The connections between superstitions and luck are well established in the minds of believers. In the cold light of reason, these associations could not be considered rational or logical. But logic and reason cannot explain luck. 'Lady luck' can be fickle and it makes sense to take every precaution to attract the good and keep away the bad, even if such behaviour appears ludicrous or primitive to others.

Miracles

A miracle (from the Latin *miraculum*, meaning 'something wonderful') is an occurrence that seems to have been caused by an act of God, or some other supernatural entity, and in which the normal workings of the laws of nature are altered, or interfered with, in some fashion. Many believers in miracles regard them as 'Divine intervention' and, if God is omnipotent, then miracles are possible. In everyday usage, the word often has a broader application, such as 'It was a miracle he escaped' or 'It is a miracle no one was killed', meaning that it was very lucky that things were not worse. In addition, something as unlikely as winning the lottery might be regarded as miraculous, as the winner has defied staggering odds.

As a miracle is something very unusual and improbable, it is easy to see why many regard it as the work of God. There are examples of miracles in the Bible, the Quran and the Hebrew Bibles, though each religion takes a different view of the phenomenon and much depends on one's interpretation of the sacred texts, or variations in translation. One such case is that of the Israelites crossing the Red Sea while escaping from Egypt. The best-known account has the Israelites crossing the Red Sea, which has parted to let them through and then closed again to trap and destroy the pursuing forces of the Pharaoh. According to one translation of the relevant passage in the Book of Exodus, a better rendition might be 'Sea of Reeds' rather than the Red Sea, and it was the wind that parted the reeds for the Israelites. Many Christians do not accept this interpretation and Hollywood movies have, understandably, been unable to resist the drama of the parting waters.

In the New Testament, there are a number of accounts of Jesus performing miracles, though St John refers to them as 'events'. Among the better known are the turning of water into wine at the wedding feast in Cana, the feeding of the multitude with five loaves and two fish, healing the blind, curing lepers and raising Lazarus from the dead. Those who have a strong faith in God, and believe in his omnipotence, accept these miracles as just another sign of His power. There are, however, many who subscribe to Christian beliefs and doctrines but have trouble accepting the authenticity of miracles. There have been attempts by some in the Catholic Church, and outside, to explain these miracles, but since miracles are, by their very nature, inexplicable in ordinary terms, such attempts would appear futile and the work of those who do not believe in miracles. As to the changing of water into wine by Jesus in Cana, sceptics suggest that perhaps the wine skins used to hold the water had earlier contained wine and had retained some of the flavour. The biblical account does not bear this out, as it states that the wine Jesus had changed was superior to the wine that had been served earlier. This was remarked upon as an unusual way of serving wine as, usually, the best wine was served first and later, when the drinkers had had their taste buds, and probably their senses, somewhat dulled, the inferior wine was served.

As to raising Lazarus from the dead, the doubter or rationaliser claims that Lazarus was not dead, but in some kind of trance or semi-conscious condition. It has even been suggested that Lazarus was participating in some kind of 'rebirth' ritual as an induction into a particular society or cult and was not really dead at all. With the blind, one can claim that they were not 'really' blind, perhaps only faking blindness to get money as beggars. With such rationalisation, the person is saying that a miracle did not take place. With miracles, one either believes or does not believe.

Followers of Islam believe that the revelation of the verses of the Quran by an angel to the Prophet Mohammed is the greatest miracle. Hindus accept the possibility of miracles and some Buddhists believe that the Buddha could perform miracles. The Catholic Church accepts miracles as the work of God, but it is very thorough in its investigation of each reported case. There are strict criteria that must be met before a miracle is given official recognition. Some Catholics, who are seen to have lived highly spiritual or exemplary lives, are considered for sainthood after their deaths. (The late Pope John Paul II is due to be declared a saint in late 2013.) The Congregation for the Causes of Saints is responsible for investigating the lives of people who may be canonised. It is common for Catholics to pray to God and the Blessed Virgin for such people. It is considered necessary for the candidate to have brought about, or be deemed to have brought about, a miracle in order to be canonised.

Perhaps the best-known miracle in relatively modern times is what has become known as the Miracle of the Sun, which took place near Fatima, Portugal, on 13 October 1907. A crowd of up to 100,000 saw, or claimed to see, the Sun perform strange movements in the sky. Observers said the Sun danced, spun around, took on different colours and then appeared to fall towards the Earth. This lasted for ten minutes. Before this strange event, there had been torrential rain that had drenched the crowd. After the Sun's strange behaviour, the people and the ground all round were dry.

It is not just religious people who believe in miracles. Some philosophers have also accepted the possibility of miracles. The writer C S Lewis, a man of beliefs as well as a deep thinker, was open to the possibility of miracles and the 17th-century Dutch philosopher Baruch Spinoza regarded miracles as occurrences for which man, in his ignorance, could not find an explanation. David Hume, an 18th-century Scottish philosopher, saw miracles as the intervention of God, or some other power, to alter or disrupt the laws of nature. Søren Kierkegaard (1813–1855) held a similar view, but cautioned that history could not always be accepted as true or correct, thus casting doubt on the accounts of miracles. This is one of the difficulties in dealing with miracles. Many of the claimed miracles happened hundreds or thousands of years ago and there is no evidence left behind to check, only the written accounts. In other cases, only a small number of people witnessed the miracles and those who do not accept the validity of miracles would be likely to be sceptical of such accounts.

Most scientists, who do not like to hear about the normal course of nature being disrupted, dismiss miracles as being impossible. Others, more cautious (or perhaps more humble), will say that miracles, if they exist, are events for which science, at least at the present, has no explanation. This viewpoint holds out the possibility that miracles do occur or that some day, when scientific knowledge is greater, an explanation may be found.

It is not easy to ignore, or dismiss, the Miracle of the Sun in Fatima, an event witnessed by a huge crowd of people. Most of us have heard of cases where patients who had been diagnosed by specialists as having terminal illnesses, and given only a short time to live, have made 'miraculous' or 'lucky' recoveries and lived on for many years. Sceptics might say that the specialist made an incorrect diagnosis, but what about all the tests, the scans and other procedures, that were carried out? Were all of them also incorrect or faulty?

As we saw earlier, lone survivors of shipwrecks, plane crashes, fires or other accidents or natural disasters, are often referred to as 'lucky' or as having had 'a miraculous escape'. Many such individuals have considered themselves not just as lucky but as having been singled out and saved for some unknown purpose. Some spend the rest of their lives trying to find this reason. In this context it is, one supposes, only natural that a person should look for some 'reason' for being so favoured by luck. One can conclude from this that such lucky escapes were just that (or miracles, if you wish) and had no further significance – or were part of some big plan.

It is not just the people who have these miraculous escapes who are lucky. Believers who have witnessed, or believe they have witnessed, a miracle will have their faith greatly strengthened and must surely be seen as luckier than those who have not had such experiences and must struggle with doubt and try to keep faith in difficult circumstances. Faith has been described as a gift. Perhaps miracles and luck are, too.

Feng Shui

Feng shui (pronounced 'fung shway') is the ancient Chinese art of endeavouring to obtain the maximum amount of Qi (energy) by uniting and balancing the laws that govern the Earth and the Heavens. A combination of geography and astronomy, it was used mainly in the choosing of sites for, and the alignment of, dwelling places and graves (the ultimate dwelling place). It was used for all buildings, from hovels to palaces, and from simple graves to splendid tombs. Archaeological studies have shown that feng shui has been used for over 6,000 years.

Using the contemporary knowledge of astronomy, the north–south axis was laid out from the positions of circumpolar stars. Before the invention of the compass, a type of astrolabe was used. The feng shui approach was what would now be called holistic. Before starting a building, the best time to do this was determined. Then the proposed site was carefully checked in relation to its immediate environment, the soil, the land and the vegetation. If a spot was considered unsuitable, then another was found. The Chinese believed that only certain places were meant to be inhabited. The aim was to find the ideal site and then build the structure at the right time, according to feng shui principles, to ensure the maximum amount of energy and luck.

The Chinese believed that what happened in the Heavens affected what happened on Earth (but not in the same way as modern astrologers) and it was therefore very advisable for people to be aware of what was happening in the heavens.

For long, feng shui and its Heaven–Earth connection was treated as superstitious Oriental nonsense by westerners – particularly missionaries, who were loud in their disapproval and condemnation. However, modern science has found that events in the Heavens, even far away, can affect the Earth, albeit not in the way the Chinese had imagined. Sunspots, magnetic storms and other celestial events can affect, among other things, electricity grids and GPS and communications equipment.

Feng shui is closely related to yin and yang, which represent, according to various interpretations, male/female, positive/negative and giving/getting. They make up the elements of feng shui – water, wood, fire, soil and metal. The objective here is to achieve harmony and equilibrium when elements complement each other or cancel each other out. The idea is similar to Horace's Golden Mean, which advocated moderation in all things, so that balance could be achieved. The same idea is found with dieticians who recommend a 'balanced' diet. A normal, well-adjusted person is called 'well-balanced' and someone who is not considered 'normal' is often referred to as 'unbalanced'.

The Chinese were keenly aware of the difference between magnetic north and true north. Their compass readings must, on occasions, have caused surprise and frustration. The Geological Survey of Canada's National Geomagnetic Program has shown that the position of magnetic north is constantly shifting and may move up to as much as 50 miles from its centre point on a given day. The magnetic compass will always point to magnetic north and other observations and calculations are needed to find true north.

Feng shui was condemned and forbidden during China's Cultural Revolution, but has made something of a comeback in recent times. Today, feng shui is more popular in the west, particularly the US, than in China. It is of interest to environmentalists, architects, geographers and members of the public alike. People who wish to build a structure or furnish it, or lay out a garden according to feng shui principles are spoilt for choice and can choose from a wide variety of feng shui schools. Interest was particularly strong after President Nixon's 1972 visit to the People's Republic of China. It is popular with New Age thinkers, who see it as a possible way of obtaining harmony, balance and peace in their dwellings.

It is very easy to dismiss feng shui (as many did) as some kind of superstitious Oriental quackery, but it should be borne in mind that the Chinese were far ahead of the west in many areas for hundreds of years. They had roads before the Romans and we must credit (or blame) them for being the earliest bureaucrats. They invented the compass and the abacus. They were also the first to use gunpowder. They were the first philosophers and came up with a 'Way' that still attracts many in the modern world. They are also well known for a strong belief in luck and a love of gambling.

Feng shui is related to luck in that those who followed its principles believed that they would obtain the maximum Qi, the positive energy, and thus be more likely to have good fortune. In their belief that certain places were not meant for human habitation, they have shown more discrimination than some modern developers who build on flood plains and other unsuitable areas, leaving as little green space as possible. People who live near volcanoes or on tectonic fault lines often become the victims of volcanic eruptions or earthquakes. We sympathise with these victims but, deep down, feel that they must know, and accept, the risks that they run. They are engaged in a gamble with the forces of nature and will sometimes lose. Those who live on low-lying islands run the risk of flooding or devastation from tsunamis. Perhaps there are simply some places where people should not live!

But it is not easy for many people to relocate and, even after a natural disaster, the survivors usually continue to live in the same area, or in close proximity. When a natural disaster claims a large number of lives, the media often prefer to concentrate on the 'miracle' or 'lucky' escapes, the people who are pulled from the rubble days after the catastrophe. The living probably provide better footage than the dead, and perhaps it is as well to concentrate on the positive and to try to give hope at a time of disaster.

Auspices and Omens
Auspices, from Latin, means 'one who looks at the birds'. In ancient Roman times, an official known as an auger would 'take the auspices' by observing the flight of birds, what kind of patterns or groups they formed and what species of birds were sighted. These auspices were regarded as a sign from the gods and were usually performed before important public events. They were an attempt to find out whether a particular time was lucky (auspicious) or unlucky (inauspicious) for an event to be held. Here again we see random, unpredictable behaviour (in this case the behaviour of birds) being regarded as a message from the gods. Of course, it all depended on how this random behaviour was interpreted by the auger. An augur could, for some personal

or political reason, or because he had been bribed, delay an event, claiming that the auspices were unfavourable for a particular time.

Romulus and Remus, the legendary founders of Rome, are said to have decided on the location of the city by taking the auspices. Romulus wanted the city built on the Palatine Hill, while Remus favoured the Aventine Hill. An argument ensued that was resolved by a contest in which they would test their abilities to auger. The one who augured the better would clearly have the approval of the gods and his site should be chosen. Plutarch tells us that Romulus spotted 12 vultures, while Remus could manage only six. The fact that Rome prospered and built up a large empire could be interpreted, by those so inclined, as proof of the efficacy of auguring.

Another way the Romans tried to tell the future was by omens. Omens were believed to portend, or presage, the future. They could be good or bad. The word 'omen' has given us 'ominous', which refers only to the bad. There were two main ways of taking the omens. The first was the auspices, the bird-watchers we have dealt with above. The second method was more hands-on and messy, carried out by an official known as a haruspex. An animal was carefully selected, then killed and its internal organs removed for examination, while the carcass was usually burned as a sacrifice to the gods. The most important organ for the haruspex was the liver. Its condition was carefully checked and, on this, the haruspex declared whether the omens were good or bad. Again, the will of the gods had been revealed to mankind, but not directly. The messages were in a form that could be read only by those who were skilled (or believed to be skilled) in such matters. The gods were telling people what was good or bad, lucky or unlucky, in the future. After all, everything was 'in the lap of the gods'. The ancients believed that the gods could, and did, sometimes take human, animal or other form, but they usually did so for their own purposes. It was not their normal custom to deliver messages personally. However, they did give signs, like birds or livers, and it was up to man to interpret these.

The Romans believed in luck and the goddess Fortuna was worshipped by many seeking good fortune. When the desire to find out the future was a matter of state, the Romans generally chose the methods described above. It was important that they were performed in public for all to see. But it was only for the augers and haruspices to interpret. This was the Roman government being 'transparent'.

Other omens were plain for all to see. Comets and eclipses were traditionally regarded as significant. Eclipses were generally regarded as bad, but comets could be interpreted in different ways. Matthew's Gospel tells us that the magi, the Three Wise Men from the East, knew of the forthcoming birth of Jesus when they saw the Star of Bethlehem (some claim it was Halley's Comet). The comet was definitely visible in 1066 at the time of the Battle of Hastings. The Bayeux tapestry shows men 'looking at the star'. As to the luck brought by the comet, an arrow killed Harold II while William the Conqueror went on to establish Norman England.

While these practices may appear quaint to us, we should remember that, while their methods were different, their aims were very similar to those modern people who 'read' tea-leaves, consult crystal balls or use psychic hotlines.

Oracles

'Oracle' can refer to an individual who is believed to give good advice or predict the future, usually because he or she is believed to be in contact with the gods. It can also refer to that advice or prediction, and even to the place where the information is given. Augury and auspice, as we have just seen, were also regarded as being oracular, as the god or goddess was believed to be sending a message through birds or some other medium.

Oracles have been used in an attempt to learn about the future or the will of the gods for over 15,000 years, showing that curiosity about what is to come is a very old trait. Rulers, or people of importance or wealth, who wanted to learn what the future held, or what they should do, often consulted oracles. On a less elevated level, a businessman or trader might consult an oracle to find out what were the prospects or portents for trade, seafaring or farming, so that they could make better-informed decisions.

A person who believed that he was experiencing extremely bad luck, or was the victim of a curse, might also consult an oracle. Ancient peoples believed that bad luck was usually the result of having offended or neglected a particular god. The visit to the oracle was to find out what, or who, was causing this bad luck and how to remedy it. It was hoped that the oracle could identify the god that had to be propitiated, or the person who had put the curse on them.

The earliest known oracle was the city of Per-Wadjet in Egypt, which is believed to have been in use in 1000 BC. It was dedicated to the worship of the god Wadjet. Later, other oracles were set up for the different Egyptian gods. While in Egypt, Alexander the Great visited a temple that was sacred to Amun. It is not known what he was told there, but some say he was informed that he was Amun's son, which cannot have hurt his self-esteem. Alexander is known to have had what would now be called a 'strained' relationship with his father, King Philip of Macedon, and would, no doubt, be delighted to hear he was the son of a powerful god.

From Egypt, oracles are believed to have spread to Greece in about 1200 BC. However, the famous temple–oracle at Dodona, that was sacred to the Mother Goddess, was said to date back to the second millennium BC, in pre-Hellenic times. Writing in the 5th century BC, Herodotus credited it with being the most ancient Hellenic oracle. More famous than Dodona, though not as old, was the oracle of Delphi. This was long known as a place of worship of Apollo, but later developed into an oracle whose fame spread far beyond the boundaries of Greece

In *Fire from Heaven*, Mary Renault gives an account of a visit to the oracle at Dodona. The pilgrim announced his presence by striking a bronze bowl with a staff. This attracted the attention of the Doves, the women who were the servants of the oracle and lived in a thatched stone hut nearby. They were always barefooted as they drew their power from the Earth.

The outcome was decided by lots, carved on small, oak tablets. The lots were in two jars – one for the god to be propitiated and the other for Yes or No. The supplicant was free to choose either jar. If the Yes/No jar was chosen, the question was placed inside, written on a piece of soft lead with a stylus. Then the Doves called an invocation. One of the Doves put her hand into the jar and drew out one of the lots. The supplicant had his answer.

At the Delphic oracle less portentous questions, such as those relating to trade or voyages, were also decided by drawing lots. For more serious matters, such as those affecting the future of states or powerful rulers, there was a more elaborate procedure. The priestess, known as the Pythia, entered the smoke-filled cave near the shrine. Here she seated herself on the tripod that was beside the Nature Stone, which was covered with magic nets. The Pythia then chewed bitter laurel as she inhaled the vapour from the rock cleft. Then she spoke her god-inspired words, mutterings that were interpreted by a priest and made into verse. These were given to the supplicant to understand as best he could. Back home, deciphering the meaning of the oracular sayings was often a protracted and contentious business. To make matters even more confused, some oracles gave out their wisdom in letters written on leaves. It was up to the supplicant to arrange the letters and interpret the message, and he had no one to blame but himself if he got it wrong.

Before deciding on his planned invasion of Asia, the aforementioned Philip of Macedon sent to the oracle at Delphi for guidance. He got the following message: 'Wreathed is the bull for the altar, the end fulfilled'. Philip was assassinated a short time after this but his son (or the son of Amun) went on to conquer much of Asia.

Another famous ruler who consulted the oracle at Delphi was Croesus, King of Lydia. He was reputed to be the richest man in the world and has given us the saying, 'As rich as Croesus'. Despite his power and great wealth, Croesus was not satisfied. He wanted to increase the size of his kingdom. He decided that he would attack the Persians but, before doing so, he took the precaution of sending to Delphi for advice and, hopefully, a prediction. In *The Histories*, Herodotus tells us that Croesus got the following message from the oracle: 'If you attack the Persians, you will destroy a great kingdom'. This was enough for Croesus. He attacked the Persians, but was routed and captured. He ended up as the adviser/captive/friend of the Persian king. A great empire had indeed been destroyed, but it was Croesus' own.

Oracles continued to operate down to 393 AD, when the Emperor Theodosius I decreed an end to 'pagan' places of worship and devotion.

Oracles were common in Europe, Asia, Africa and South America. Some continue to operate today. In Nigeria, the Igbo still consult oracles, where a priest in a trance, or ecstasy, gives prophecies or advice. The Aztecs and Maya were known to have used oracles. A Mayan oracle had even predicted the Spanish conquerors and the evils that would follow. From Norse mythology, we learn that Odin consulted an oracle and had to give one of his eyes in exchange for the wisdom he received.

India and Tibet also have a long tradition of using oracles. In 1959, the 14th Dalai Lama, leader of Tibetan Buddhists, fled Tibet and now lives in exile in Dharamsala in northern India. Tibet has an official oracle, called the Nechung Oracle, which it was customary for the Dalai Lama to visit during the Losar celebrations to usher in the Tibetan New Year.

Irrespective of religion or geographical location, people have had a long association with oracles. It is a testament to their feelings of helplessness, of being the tools of forces over which they have no control, of being the victim of bad luck, or the darling of the gods. Man was the plaything of the gods (Shakespeare's 'flies to wanton boys'), and his best hope of good fortune was to appease and cajole the gods and other spirits with sacrifices and offerings. Man felt helpless in the face of an unknown and uncertain future, and we can hardly blame him for trying to find out as much as possible about that future and how he should approach it. Oracles were consulted in the hope, or expectation, that this could be achieved. Similar services are offered today, but in this technological age, there is no need to travel to some oracle, much less watch birds or examine the entrails of animals. It can all be done online, from 'the comfort of your own home'. The telephone or the Internet connects us to the gods, or at least those 'go-betweens' who claim to have special channels to knowledge hidden from lesser mortals.

The Fates
Originally, the Fates may have been just one composite goddess. In *The Iliad*, Homer refers only to the Moirai, the controllers of the threads of men's lives, and it was only the Fates that represented Birth and Death that were worshipped in Delphi.

The Muses
In ancient Greece, the Muses were believed to inspire mythologies, literature and the arts. They were regarded as the source of knowledge, and only those who were favoured by the Muses were given this knowledge. Those fortunate people were then able to create myths, poetry, music, drama and dance. Even today, people who are talented in these areas are often seen as gifted, given a talent that they hone with practice and dedication.

In the *Theogony*, Hesiod (7th century BC) wrote that the Muses were the daughters of Zeus and Mnemosyne, the goddess of memory. Other accounts say they were the offspring of Uranus and Gaia. Each of the nine Muses had her own domain and was usually represented in sculpture and paintings by an emblem which helped to identify them.

Muse	Domain	Emblem
Calliope	Epic poetry	Writing tablet
Clio	History	Scrolls
Erato	Lyric poetry	Cithara (lyre-like instrument)
Euterpe	Song and elegiac poetry	Aulos (flute-like instrument)
Melpomene	Tragedy	Tragic mask
Polyhymnia	Choral poetry	Veil
Terpsichore	Dance	Lyre
Thalia	Comedy	Comic mask
Urania	Astronomy	Compass, globe

Many ancient, and even later, writers, opened works with an invocation or address to the Muse. Herodotus named each of the nine books of *The Histories* after a Muse and each is invoked in turn. In Book I of *The Odyssey*, Homer begins by addressing the Muse –

Sing to me of the man, Muse, the man of twists and turns, driven time and again off course, once he had plundered the hollowed heights of Troy.

(Robert Fagle translation, 1996)

Virgil opens Book I of *The Aeneid*:

O Muse! The causes and the crimes relate;
What goddess was provok'd, and whence her hate;
For what offence the queen of Heav'n began
To persecute so brave, so just a man
(John Dryden translation, 1670)

In Book II of *Troilus and Criseyde*, Geoffrey Chaucer begins:

O lady myn, that called art Cleo,
Thou be my speed fro this forth, and my Muse,
To ryme wel this book til I have do

And the Prologue of Shakespeare's *Henry V* begins with the Chorus:

> O for a Muse of fire, that would ascend
> The brightest heaven of invention!

Even some modern writers, most notably Robert Graves, pay homage to the muse. Artists, musicians or writers who produce sublime works are born, no doubt, with special talents. The Bible says that certain people are born with certain gifts. Of course, application and dedication are required to develop these talents but, without the inspiration, the spark, work and application will not produce works of genius. Not all who have been given such talents regard them as a blessing. Many are haunted, driven individuals, sometimes on the verge of insanity, possessed by their muse or demon.

Hubris

Nowadays, 'hubris' is used to refer to excessive pride or arrogance and, by extension, the retribution that sometimes follows it. In ancient Greece, where the word originated, it meant 'to get what is deserved', a slightly different meaning. It referred to actions that were intended to humiliate a victim, such as the taunting or further shaming of a defeated opponent. It was a bit like kicking a man when he was down. It also had a wider application and included deeds which seemed to oppose or defy the gods, or to go against the laws of nature (such as matricide, patricide or fratricide). It also included such crimes as sexual assault, rape, crimes that caused grievous bodily harm, and stealing objects or offerings that were considered sacred to the gods. Mutilating or otherwise dishonouring a dead body (particularly a dead hero) was also regarded as a hubristic act. The saying 'Pride goes before a fall' sums up hubris. Such deeds usually led to catastrophic results, particularly in Greek tragedies.

Nemesis was the goddess who dispensed divine justice to those guilty of hubris. She was relentless in her duty and no wrongdoer went unpunished. She brought down the proud and humbled the arrogant. Before the Greek tragedies, Nemesis was regarded as the giver of fortune. In this capacity, she was thought to be the dispenser of good and bad luck, according to what each person deserved. During the Roman imperial era, she was personified as Invidia or Pax-Nemesis. Victorious Roman generals, marching through Rome with the captives and other spoils of victory, were warned not to be too proud, to remember they were mortal, and not to commit hubris. The wise ones were careful to worship her and offer sacrifice, lest they draw down her punishment. Gladiators also worshipped her.

Nemesis had the assistance of the Furies. Known to the Greeks as Erinyes (angry ones) or Eumenides (grim ones), they also dispensed vengeance or retribution. They are usually presented as being three in number – Tisiphone (vengeful destruction), Megaera (jealousy and envy) and Alecto (unceasing anger). At times they are portrayed as hideous creatures with Gorgon-like snakes for hair and blood coming from their eyes, and on other occasions as bat-like harpies.

There are numerous examples of hubris in Homer. After Achilles had killed the Trojan warrior Hector, he dragged the body of the fallen hero behind his chariot and, for long, refused to return it to his family for burial. In the end, Achilles relented and gave the body to Priam, the King of Troy and Hector's broken-hearted father. However, it was too late for Achilles. He had committed hubris and he did not leave Troy alive.

Xerxes I, King of the Persians, was regarded by the Greeks as being punished by Nemesis. At the Battle of Salamis in 480 BC, the mighty Persian force was defeated by the Greeks. The defeat of General Custer and the 7th Cavalry at the Battle of the Little Bighorn is regarded by some in the same light, as is the failure of the 1588 Spanish Armada and Napoleon Bonaparte's disastrous invasion of Russia in 1812.

Ulysses
On the long and arduous voyage from Troy to his home in Ithaca, Ulysses (the Roman name, known as Odysseus in Greek) and his crew were captured by the Cyclops, Polyphemus, and imprisoned in his cave with his sheep. When asked his name by the Cyclops, Ulysses, known for his cunning, replied 'Nobody'. While the Cyclops was sleeping, Ulysses and his companions blinded his one eye with a heated stake. When Polyphemus called out to the other Cyclopes 'He is attacking me', there was a reply from another Cyclops in a nearby cave: 'Who is attacking you?' 'Nobody is attacking me,' came the response.

Later, Ulysses and his men escaped from the cave strapped under the bellies of the sheep. Once outside, they unstrapped themselves and lost no time in getting to their ship. Safely aboard, and thinking himself out of danger, Ulysses could not resist the temptation of taunting the blinded Cyclops. This angered Polyphemus, who threw huge missiles at the departing ship and almost sank it. Ulysses and his crew managed to escape, but they had made a powerful enemy. By adding insult to injury, Ulysses angered the Cyclops' father – who just happened to be Poseidon, god of the sea. Poseidon, who was already angry with Ulysses for not making sacrifice to him when he had saved him from detection inside the Wooden Horse at Troy, was in no mood to forgive and forget. On his voyage, Ulysses encountered many difficulties. All his men perished and Ulysses was very lucky to make it home alive.

All the trouble that he had, not just on his voyage home but also at Troy, did not come as a surprise to Ulysses. Before leaving home for Troy, he had been told by an oracle that, if he left Ithaca, he would not see home again for 20 years. He had done everything possible to avoid going to Troy with Agamemnon and the other warriors, but in the end he had to go. The oracle was right. He spent ten years in Troy and ten years trying to get home. Even when he got home, his troubles were not over. A gang of suitors swarmed around his wife, Penelope. They told her that her husband was dead and that she should marry again. Not knowing if her husband was dead or alive, she was in a quandary. The suitors were offensive and at times insistent, and were eating Penelope and her son, Telemachus, out of house and home. Penelope managed to fend them off with promises and stratagems until Ulysses returned. The suitors had committed hubris and Homer shows no sympathy for them when they were killed by Ulysses and his son. Nemesis had done her work.

Oedipus

The dominant theme of Greek tragic drama was that there was no way the hero could avoid his fate. The fate that was laid down for him by the Fates was inescapable – it did not take a hubristic act for tragedy to befall the hero. In Oedipus, we meet a tragic hero who, despite his best efforts, cannot escape his fate. His sad tale is told by Sophocles in three plays – *Oedipus the King*, *Antigone* and *Oedipus at Colonus*. The Fates were generally thought to determine a person's life when they were three days old but, in the case of Oedipus, it seems they could not wait and had decided even before he was born. Before Oedipus (which means, 'swollen foot') was born, his father, King Laius of Thebes, and mother, Queen Jocasta, were told by an oracle that their son would kill his father and later marry his mother. In order that the prophecy would not be fulfilled, when Oedipus was born, Laius had his ankles pierced and his feet bound (the cause of the 'swollen feet'). Then the child was left out on a hill to die. As luck would have it, Oedipus was found by a shepherd and taken to the palace of King

Polybus in Corinth, where he grew up thinking Polybus was his father. However, the day came when he learned, some say from a drunk, that Polybus was not his father. When he confronted the king with this news, Polybus insisted that he was his father. Not satisfied with this, Oedipus consulted an oracle and was told his future. He was fated to kill his father and later marry his mother. To prevent this from happening, Oedipus left Corinth and decided to go to Thebes.

On the way, he met a chariot at a crossroads. There was an argument over who had right of way, a fight broke out, and Oedipus killed the charioteer, who happened to be his father, King Laius. Further on along the road, Oedipus met the Sphinx, whose habit was to stop all travellers and ask them to answer the following riddle – 'What walks on four legs in the morning, two at noon and three in the evening?' Travellers who had been unable to give the correct answer became a snack for the Sphinx, and no one yet had given the correct answer. Oedipus was up to the challenge. 'Man,' he answered, adding how a child crawled on all four, an adult walked on two legs and the old needed a stick to get around. Infuriated that her riddle had been answered, the Sphinx hurled herself off a cliff.

As a result of getting rid of the Sphinx, Oedipus became a hero in Thebes. Before long he married the widow, Jocasta (whose husband he had killed at the crossroads) and, in the course of time, had four children. A few years after the marriage, there was a plague in Thebes. The hero, Oedipus, vowed to stop it. The queen's brother, Creon, was sent to the oracle at Delphi, and came back with the news that the person who had killed King Laius had to be found and punished. But, how was the killer to be found? The oracle had not given this information. Creon had an idea. He advised Oedipus to seek out Tiresias, the blind seer, who was half man and half woman. When contacted, Tiresias was very reluctant to name the killer, but was eventually persuaded. When he got the answer, Oedipus began to see the horror of his situation. Looking around for someone to blame, he accused Creon of giving Tiresias the information. His wife/mother, Jocasta, tried to put his mind at rest and Creon now became the villain of the piece. Oedipus was not sure who to believe, but was beginning to think that he had killed King Laius. Then word came that King Polybus of Corinth was dead. Oedipus still believed that Polybus was his father, but the messenger who brought the news of the death also told that, before he died, Polybus had admitted that Oedipus was adopted. The truth had now dawned on Jocasta and she entreated Oedipus to give up the search for Laius' killer. Unfortunately, Oedipus did not understand what she was trying to tell him. In desperation, Jocasta went away and hanged herself.

Still not believing the story of his adoption by Polybus, Oedipus found the herdsman who had been told to leave him on the hillside to die. From him he learned the truth and was struck by the reality of his situation – the man he had killed at the crossroads was his father, King Laius, and Jocasta, the woman he had married, had been the wife of Laius, and his mother. The prophecies of the oracle had been fulfilled. Oedipus then went to look for Jocasta and learned that she had hanged herself. In despair, he gouged out his eyes with a brooch he removed from her gown. His uncle/brother-in-law, Creon, was magnanimous and Oedipus left Thebes, with his daughter Antigone. They went from place to place until, eventually, King Theseus of Athens granted then permission to live at Colonus, where Oedipus died some time later.

The moral of the story is clear. A person cannot change or escape his fate. Most people would agree that Oedipus was particularly unlucky. The misfortune that befell him was not caused by him knowingly doing what was wrong. In fact, he made every effort to avoid what had been predicted for him. The Fates had been particularly unkind to him.

Agamemnon
We feel sorry for Oedipus because he did not seem to deserve what happened to him. In the case of Agamemnon, we are less likely to be sympathetic, as he brought his misfortune down on himself. Many would conclude that he got what he deserved, but the ancients were much more generous in their appraisal of him.

In *Agamemnon* by Aeschylus, we learn of the fate of the hero of Troy, to whom Homer usually refers as the 'leader of men'. Agamemnon was the King of Mycenae and the brother of Menelaus, King of Sparta, whose wife (Helen) Paris had taken away to his home in Troy. Agamemnon, eager to extend his kingdom, used the case of Helen as a pretext to attack Troy. He assembled a large army and prepared to set out for Troy. However, the winds were not favourable and he was becalmed in Aulis. He became impatient, as did his men, and he was afraid that his alliance might fall apart if he did not set sail soon. Agamemnon had earlier offended the goddess Artemis by killing an animal that was sacred to her. To make matters worse, he had later boasted about it. The seer, Calchas, told Agamemnon that if he was to appease Artemis and get a favourable wind, he must sacrifice his daughter, Iphigenia. The girl was lured to Aulis in the belief that she was to be married to Achilles. Once in Aulis she was led to the altar and sacrificed by her father. Shortly afterwards, the wind changed and they sailed for Troy.

Back home in Mycenae, Agamemnon's wife, Clytemnestra – who was of a different stamp than Ulysses' faithful Penelope – was horrified and infuriated by the sacrifice of her daughter. With her boyfriend, Aegisthus, she planned to get her revenge. It did not help matters when, ten years later, Agamemnon returned from Troy with Cassandra, the daughter of King Priam of Troy, as a spoil of war. According to Aeschylus, Clytemnestra tried to trick her husband into committing hubris by walking on a purple tapestry that was reputed to have been woven by the gods. Had Agamemnon trodden on the tapestry, his action would have been seen as desecration and an insult to the gods, who would surely have called on Nemesis, or the Furies, to deal with him. Clytemnestra had hoped the gods would do her dirty work for her. But Agamemnon did not fall for it and she had to take matters into her own hands. Along with the help of Aegisthus, she killed Agamemnon. Some accounts say she killed him during a banquet, while others say she killed him while he was having a bath.

His son, Orestes, now had the duty to avenge his father's death. Apollo had told him to do so, but to do this he would have to commit matricide, a crime punished by Nemesis and/or the Furies. Nevertheless he killed Aegisthus and his mother and, as a result, was hounded by the Furies. Orestes prayed to Apollo for assistance but it was the goddess Athena who interceded for him with the Furies.

As in the case of Oedipus, we see here characters that are trapped by their fates and seem to have little choice, though we feel more sympathy for Oedipus and Orestes than for Agamemnon.

Even in modern times, hubris and nemesis seem to be still with us, at least in some cases. The boy-racer who has been doing doughnuts or some other reckless manoeuvres and then crashes his car would be seen as 'getting what he deserved' and that it 'was good enough for him'. His foolish showing-off has brought its just punishment. While no one would like to see the young fellow killed or seriously injured, a few bruises and a lot of embarrassment might not seem undeserved. However, were you to take this attitude towards the boy-racer, then you to might risk committing hubris in that you were taking some pleasure in another's misfortune.

There are times when the world seems to be very unjust, when the guilty are rewarded and the innocent punished, and we long for some kind of justice or retribution. We see kleptocrats who get away scot-free with the help of expensive lawyers, corrupt politicians who use their power to protect themselves from prosecution, and rich people who flaunt their wealth in a world where millions die every year from malnutrition or starvation. It is only natural that we would hope for Nemesis to take a hand, but we need to know where justice ends and vengeance begins.

Numerology
Numerology is a belief system in which there is thought to be a connection between numbers and the other elements in the universe, such as objects and people. It dates back to the time of Pythagoras, who regarded numbers as the most direct and practical way of understanding the universe. The tradition continued down through the mysteries of the early Christian Church, but the first Church Council of Nicea, in 325, placed numerology in the category of unacceptable beliefs and, as such, it was classified with astrology and other 'pagan' practices. However, the view of the council did not gain general acceptance and St Augustine of Hippo (354–430), one of the most influential of the early theologians, was in agreement with Pythagoras and felt it was valid and permissible to look for the meanings behind numbers. 'Numbers are the universal language offered by the deity to humans as confirmation of the truth,' he wrote. Because of the fixed values of numbers, it was felt they could ascertain and confirm the truth, and did not lend themselves as easily as words to many and varied interpretations.

Interest in numerology has fluctuated during the course of history, but it never disappeared. Today, there are many who believe that numbers are mystical and point to, or produce, good or bad luck. This is particularly so in Chinese numerology.

In China, the belief that a number is lucky or unlucky was usually based on the sound of the number and what other words it resembled. As there are a number of dialects in Chinese, the same numbers may not be regarded as lucky, or unlucky, in all areas. Despite this, it is possible to make some generalisations. The Chinese proverb, 'Good things come in pairs', means that even numbers are usually regarded as lucky, while odd numbers are counted unlucky – but not always. Most odd numbers between one and ten are not considered particularly unlucky. In fact, the unluckiest number is the even number, four, as it sounds like the word for 'death'. The odd number, three, sounds like 'live', and is, therefore, regarded as lucky. Two is lucky (a pair) and eight is considered particularly lucky, as it sounds like the word 'prosper'. As a result, car number plates, identity cards, or personal identity numbers that contain many eights are regarded as very lucky and wealthy Chinese are prepared to pay huge sums of money to acquire them. Nick Leeson, the Singapore-based 'rogue trader' at Barings Bank, created account number 888 for his illegal (but eventually disastrous) transactions. By the same token, no one wants the number four in their car registration, identity documents or telephone number. Strangely, zero is considered lucky as it sounds like 'everything'. Nine, the highest of the single digit numbers, is also regarded as lucky because it sounds like 'longevity'.

The number eight played a big part in deciding the moment of the opening of the Summer Olympic Games in Beijing. They began at eight seconds past eight minutes past eight o'clock on the eighth day of the eighth month in the year 2008. Chinese athletes did very well.

It is only to be expected that, when choosing numbers for lotteries, there will be a general preference for 'lucky' numbers, though probability tells us that all numbers would have an equal chance of winning. When trying to pick winning numbers, some people believe that if they select the numbers by some arcane or convoluted procedure, the numbers that emerge are likely to be luckier. To them, it seems a more likely way of picking winners than just selecting at random. One method is to take a word and give its letters numerical values. A simple method would be to assign the letter A the numerical value 1, B would be 2, C 3, and so on up to the number 9. The tenth letter of the alphabet, J, would again be 1, K would represent 2 and L 3. After going through the entire alphabet, a person would end up with the following:

1 = A, J and S   2 = B, K and T   3 = C, L and U   4 = D, M and V
5 = E, N and W   6 = F, O and X   7 = G, P and Y   8 = H, Q and Z   9 = I and R

As stated above, this is a very simple system and anyone can create any other system they fancy. For example, you could start at the other end and assign 9 to A, 8 to B and so on. For those who wish to use established systems, there are the Hebrew, Greek and Armenian systems.

Let's go back to our first system and see how it works when one is trying to select 'lucky' numbers for a lottery with, say, 50 numbers in the drum or bubble. One would first select a word – let's say the word 'lucky' – which would give the values 3+3+3+2+7 = 18. So, 18 is your first 'lucky' number. You look more closely and notice that the letters C, L and U all have the value 3. Is that significant? Is the word 'lucky', lucky? How about the word 'win'? This gives 5+5+9 = 19. There's your second 'lucky' number. Is it a coincidence that it is the next number after the first number you have obtained? You recall that two consecutive numbers often come up in lotteries. In addition, to make things even better, two of the letters, N and W, both have the value 5. You seem to be doing well! You continue and select more numbers. Were you to select a word whose numerical value added up to more than 50, what are you to do? No problem. Say you end up with 57. You can add the two numbers and get 12 or, if you prefer, subtract them and get 2, whichever you feel is 'luckier'. To get a single-digit number, one can add or subtract other numbers as chance prompts them.

By going through such routines, some people will convince themselves that the time and effort put into the process is likely to come up with 'luckier' numbers than those just chosen off the top of the head. In a way, they feel that the effort put into selecting the numbers means they deserve to win. Certainly, they will feel they are more deserving than a person who does a quick-pick/'lucky dip' and lets the computer do the choosing. This holds true even for some people who have an understanding of randomness. When they hear that a person with a quick-pick has won a large amount of money, they feel it is somehow unfair, as that person had not used any 'skill' in selecting the numbers. They regard the person as 'just lucky' and as having done nothing to help attract or 'wake-up' their luck. Unfortunately, all this does nothing to affect randomness or probability.

The Big Bang

The Book of Genesis states that, 'In the beginning, God created the heaven and the earth', without telling us when that act of creation took place. The Catholic Church, using the Bible as the foundation of its beliefs, took the words of Genesis as gospel, and did not encourage questions that might seem to challenge, or doubt, its veracity or authenticity. The Earth was believed to be flat and the centre of the Solar System, with the Sun orbiting around it. Galileo got into trouble with the Church authorities for suggesting that things might be otherwise and it was not until Copernicus that the Earth lost its central position and was relegated to being just another planet ('wanderer' in Greek) orbiting the Sun.

Early man was very interested in the innumerable heavenly bodies he could see above him on a dark, starry night. What he learned served not only as the basis of astrology, but also as a means of determining direction. Clusters, or groups, of stars were given names like The Plough, The Big Dipper, Orion and The Great Bear, as they were regarded as resembling objects, animals or heroes of the Earth.

For a very long time, man was more interested in studying the heavens above than the Earth beneath his feet. There seems to have been little curiosity about the age of the Earth, how its inhabitants came to be there and what forces had shaped it and them. It was seen as the creation of God and taken as such without too much enquiry. But after the Renaissance, when man woke up from the Dark Ages, he began to use reason and logic as ways of attempting to understand what was around him. There was confidence that the world was knowable and that man had the ability to do so.

In that context, it is rather surprising that it was not a scientist, or freethinker, who was the first to try to calculate the age of the Earth, to find out when exactly 'the beginning' was. It was an Anglican Archbishop called James Ussher (1581–1656) who first attempted to calculate the Earth's age. Usher was the Church of Ireland Archbishop of Armagh and Primate of All Ireland from 1625 to 1656. A man of erudition and a respected academic, he worked backwards through history, assigning dates to certain events, such as the assassination of Julius Caesar in 44 BC, and the death of Alexander the Great in 323 BC. Back to the time of King Nebuchadnezzar of Babylon, he was on fairly solid, historical ground, but before that time, events and personalities were less easy to date. One difficulty was to determine the length of time that had elapsed between Creation and the Flood. He had calculated that the Temple of Solomon had been built 3,000 years after Creation and 1,000 years before the birth of Christ. That gave a creation date of 4,000 years before the birth of Christ in the year 4 BC. But Ussher was much more specific than that. In his 1654 work *Annalium pars posterior*, he gave the date of creation as being nightfall preceding 23 October 4004 BC. While we may smile knowingly at his date, we must remember that Ussher was working with the best information available in the first half of the 17th century, and he was correct in dating the deaths of Julius Caesar and Alexander.

Ussher's date was generally accepted until, with the discoveries in the burgeoning sciences of geology and palaeontology, it began to appear that the Earth was much older than the good cleric had stated. As science progressed and knowledge increased, the continued efforts of scientists, in a number of disciplines that related to the age of the Earth and the universe, began to yield concrete results. Based on radiometric age and the dating of meteoric material, they eventually came up with the figure of approximately 4.5 billion years.

As time moved on, man's curious and ever-probing mind began to reach even further back in time in an attempt to determine the age of the universe, which, all the evidence showed, was much older than the Earth. Just finding out when the universe began would not satisfy them – they also wanted to know how it happened. With the development of more sophisticated astronomical equipment, cosmologists began to look for evidence that might lead to answers. The most widely-accepted theory they have come up with so far is that known as the Big Bang.

As the Big Bang has sometimes been credited with (or blamed for) everything that has happened in the universe since that time, according to determinism and the significance of initial conditions, it might be of interest to take a brief look at it. A Belgian Catholic priest, Georges Lemaître, first propounded the theory in 1927. Two years later, the astronomical observations of Edwin Hubble gave further credence to the theory, as did Einstein's work on relativity. The theory holds that, at the moment of the Big Bang, there was just one atom, which Lemaître called a 'primal atom', from which the entire universe has evolved. Space and time did not exist before the Big Bang. It would be incorrect to imagine space as existing beforehand as a void, waiting to be filled. Some scientists have compared space to a giant rubber mat that expanded as the giant explosion propelled everything outwards. Time, also, did not exist. Time is closely related to the other dimensions and is, basically, a measure of change. Before the Big Bang, there was no change to measure. The Big Bang theory is unable to explain, at least at this time, the initial condition, but it does offer a description and explanation of what happened very, very shortly afterwards.

There is a huge bang. Time and space comes into existence. From a very, very short time after this bang – in fact about ten to the power of minus eleven seconds after – cosmologists are confident they can tell what happened. They say that the energy of the particles decreased, with the result that protons and neutrons began to form. The universe began to cool and grow bigger. All this is believed to have happened 13.7 billion years ago. Since then the universe has been expanding. Not only is it expanding, but it seems that the expansion is accelerating, still using the energy of the Big Bang. Over the course of time stars, planets, galaxies and other bodies have developed and moved through the universe, all propelled by the force of the Big Bang.

So, that is how it all started, but how will it all end? Indeed, will it all end? Here there are at least two, opposing, views. One theory, or hypothesis, states that the universe will keep on expanding, becoming ever bigger. Others speak of the Big Crunch. They say that, when all the energy of the Big Bang is exhausted, the universe will begin to shrink and collapse in on itself, possibly ending up again as a 'primeval atom'. Then the whole process might start all over again. Not that we are likely to be around to witness it. Long before any of this happens, the Earth will have been burnt up by the Sun as it becomes a Red Giant. Unless we have found another home by that time, things will look bad for mankind.

For those who believe in a deterministic universe, the moment of the Big Bang is very significant. This is when it all began, and since that time, everything that has happened in the universe has been following in a cause-and-effect chain that began at that moment. As the Big Bang was the first cause, it is regarded as acausal, as it is not the effect (result) of an earlier cause. So, everything follows from that first cause and the effect that followed it, right down to the present moment. Determinists, who believe the universe operates according to the laws of nature and science, say that everything that has happened, is happening or will ever happen is the result of this giant explosion. From this, it follows that nothing can be done to alter it, as everything has been predetermined. So, the person who believes he is blessed with good fortune or cursed with bad luck will have to look back to the Big Bang to find out why it is so, because his fate was decided then. If one believes this, it would be very easy to become fatalistic. Not many take such an extreme view, and the spectrum of opinions on the matter range, as we have seen, from those who believe they have no control over their lives to those who believe in complete freedom of choice. The latter will say that there is no such thing as random chance, or luck, good or bad.

The way we view time is important in how we regard the future, and how it is connected to the past and the future. Time began with the Big Bang. We divide time into three parts – the past, present and future. The past is fixed and gone, the future is out there waiting to become the present, in time. Within this, time is seen as 'moving' or 'flowing' from the past, through the present, to the future. Many thinkers have wrestled with the nature of time. St Augustine found it an elusive concept. He said that if not asked about time, he knew what it was, but if someone asked him, he could not say what it was. He thought that only the present exists. The past could be remembered, or experienced, only in the present and the future could be thought of only in the present. Both past and future existed only in the present. But what is the present? The Theory of Relativity postulates that there is no specific instant in universal time that could be called 'the present'. We believe that 'time passes', but without really knowing what time is, how can we measure its passage? How do we know how quickly it passes? Of course, there are clocks and calendars that measure time, but these are just arbitrary measurements, drawn up for our own convenience and based on the rotation of the Earth and its orbit around the Sun. The division of time into hours, minutes and seconds is just for our purposes, and tells us little about the nature of time. If you tell a person who has never seen a clock or watch that an hour has passed, he will not know what you mean, but he will understand that the position of the Sun has changed.

It is the same when talking about a year. It is a convenient unit of measurement in that the Earth takes 365.25 days to orbit the Sun. We have subdivided this year into months, weeks, days and hours for the purpose of regulating our lives and being able to refer to particular times. Such phrases as 'Time flew' or 'The time really dragged' show how subjective our perception of 'the passage of time' can be. Ten minutes spent open-mouthed in a dentist's chair will likely feel longer than ten minutes watching your favourite soccer team on television while consuming your favourite beverage. The watch on your wrist will measure time at the same rate on both occasions, but your 'internal clock' will not. When a person becomes engrossed in something they 'lose track of time', and when they subsequently look at their watch, they will exclaim, 'Is that the time?'

To complicate matters further, clocks in different places do not keep the same time. A clock on a spacecraft travelling at a speed approaching that of light, would slow down significantly. A clock on the orbiting Space Shuttle will run slower than one on the surface of the Earth.

J M E McTaggart, in his 1908 book *The Unreality of Time*, writes of two kinds of time, which he calls A-series and B-series. A-series is the normal view of time as past, present and future. B-series describes events as before and after. He rejects both models, A-series as being incoherent and B-series as not providing a sufficient understanding of time. Based on this, he concluded that time was unreal. Einstein, the man who did more than any other scientist to understand time and its scientific implications, would not have disagreed with him. In a letter of condolence to the relative of a dead friend, he referred to time as 'an illusion, but a persistent one'.

Science has come to regard time as a dimension and has added it to the other three of length, width and height to come up with what they call space-time. How quickly time passes depends on the location in the universe with which we are dealing, so scientists regard it as a variable, not a constant. Eternalists' view of time complicates matters further by speaking of an arrow of time. To them, the ticking of a watch is not measuring time, merely the duration between events.

If time is modelled in physics as another dimension, then it will have the same ontology as space. In that case, future events are already there and there is no objective flow of time as we understand it. Called 'Block Time' or 'Block Universe', space-time is seen as a 'block' with four dimensions, not a three-dimensional space that the passage of time modulates. The conventional view of time – with its past, present and future – talks of a 'passage' of time that makes the present past and the future present. Special relatively tells us that, as we stated earlier, in universal time there is no particular moment that could be called the present all over the universe. Observers in different reference frames could be said to have their own 'flow of time'. No particular observer could claim that his present was more valid than that of another. To complicate matters further, according to the Theory of Relatively, time can 'flow' at different rates.

Eternalism accepts the idea of past, present and future, but regards them as directions, not states of being. As one can remember the past but not the future, subjectively one feels that there has been a passage of time. Like determinism, eternalism says that there is no free will, that the future is as fixed and unchangeable as the past.

Many philosophers do not accept eternalism. One of the objections they put forward is that if the flow of time did not exist objectively – i.e. was just a subjective illusion – then it would be possible to experience all moments of our lives simultaneously. St Augustine believed that God was outside time and would perceive time in a different way than finite mortals. Perhaps He would regard time in the manner of the Block Time or Block Universe just mentioned, as only He would have an overall view of the universe.

This has implications for those who believe that they can change their luck. If the future is as fixed as the past, you cannot influence or change it. What is laid out for you is what you will get. Even if you think you have taken measures that have changed your luck, it could be that you were just doing what you are meant to do. Although time may be 'an illusion', we are still stuck in the present and must wait for the future to become the present before we can know it. That seems to be the way things are, unless we can travel into the future – which, many scientists claim, is impossible.

It might be some small consolation for those who feel they are experiencing what Shakespeare called 'outrageous fortune' to learn that they may be doing better, or even worse, on another universe. Some scientists have put forward the hypothesis that we should be thinking in terms of parallel universes that combine to form a 'multiverse'. The anthropic principle states that the Earth seems to have been specially made for intelligent life. That means us, or so we think. Many take this as proof that God created the Heavens and the Earth for us. In support of this opinion, they quote Isaiah 45:18 – 'He who fashioned and made the Earth, he furnished it: he did not create it to be empty, but formed it to be inhabited'. We live on a planet that is not only friendly to life, but also conducive to it. Were our universe different in its laws or composition, it is very unlikely that any life would exist on it. When we think of all that has happened in the universe in the 13.7 billion years since the Big Bang, and that we now find ourselves on a planet that seems to be fine-tuned for us, it must really make us wonder. We would have to wonder even more when we think that, based on the Rare Earth Hypothesis (of which more later), it is all the result of many improbable outcomes and random occurrences.

The multiverse hypothesis would help to explain our presence on the Earth as, if there were a large number of universes (some scientists say an infinite number), the probability of our planet and its life forms would be greatly increased. One view is that all the universes are similar, but not identical, and that we exist on all of them, but in slightly different ways. It also ties in with our views on fairness and justice, not that these have to be universal concepts. In this particular universe, a person may be experiencing a very unpleasant existence, but this will be balanced out in other universes where that person is successful and happy. Indeed, were there an infinite number of universes and we existed in all of them, then each individual would perforce experience all forms of existence, from the worst to the best. It would probably also balance out one's luck in the coin toss. If two outcomes are equally probable, as in the coin toss, there is no specific reason why one outcome rather than another should occur. In the multiverse, it will come up heads in half the universes and tails in the other half. It is just a matter of your being in the right universe at the right time. Being in the right place at the right time is a large part of luck.

The multiverse hypothesis sounds rather fanciful, and a person who is having a difficult time on this Earth, in this universe, will gain no practical advantage from being told that he is enjoying a better life in some other universe. It is also very speculative, and critics of the multiverse hypothesis point out that many of its claims lack proof and may, indeed, be unprovable. So there are two major difficulties with the hypothesis – it cannot be proved and it cannot be disproved.

Quantum physics has been around for about 100 years and in that time has established a very good record of getting things right or, at least, not being proven wrong. The type of multiverse that would be consistent with quantum mechanics would be one in which all the universes were identical in structure and laws, but in different states. In addition, the universes would not be in contact with each other, or affect each other.

The idea of the multiverse is not new. In fact, it is very old. The Puranas, and other Hindu texts, suggest the existence of an infinite number of universes. Each universe has its gods, life forms and the same cycle of birth, death and rebirth. The cycle of each universe is said to be 8.4 billion years, a figure that is less than the age of the universe but older than our Earth.

If there are a vast number of universes out there in space, and they are all different, then it would make the existence of our unique (as far as we know) and improbable planet more probable, as all possibilities would be more likely to be realised.

Rare Earth Hypothesis

Carl Sagan, Frank Drake and a number of other scientists tell us that the Earth is just an ordinary planet, going around in an ordinary system, in a typical galaxy. They say that there is nothing exceptional or unique about planet Earth, and that there may be millions or billions of similar planets in the universe, all with complex life.

Peter Ward, a palaeontologist and geologist, and Donald E Brownlee, an astronomer and astrobiologist, have a different view. In their excellent book *Rare Earth: Why Complex Life Is Uncommon in the Universe* they argue that Earth-like planets that could support complex life are few and far between. The Rare Earth hypothesis postulates that the evolution of complex, multicellular life forms is a very rare and improbable event. For such complex life to develop, the hypothesis states, a bewildering array of cosmological, chemical and geological occurrences had to take place to get us to where we are now.

According to Ward and Brownlee, for complex life to evolve a large number of criteria have to be satisfied. The planet must be in an area that can support life. It should be of a particular size, near a star of a specific type and at a suitable distance from it, and the planet should have a magnetosphere, among other things. In the vastness of the universe (or multiverse), there may be, and probably are, many planets like the Earth, but it would have to satisfy many other requirements, and have exactly the right proportion of certain critical variables, were it to qualify as a home for complex life.

The authors argue that much of the universe is made up of uninhabitable, hostile areas which they call 'dead zones'. To begin with, the further a star is from the centre of a galaxy, the less likely it is to have metals, which are needed for the formation of a life-friendly planet. (Astronomers classify all elements apart from helium and hydrogen as metals.) If there were a black hole anywhere in the vicinity, the gamma ray radiation that it emits would be so intense that it is very unlikely that complex life could evolve. So this effectively rules out areas that are too far from the centre of a galaxy as well as areas affected by a black hole or neutron star.

Another advantage of being far away from the centre of a galaxy is that there is less likelihood of being hit by something large. Having your planet impacted by a large body from space is not a good thing, as the dinosaurs found out 65 million years ago. A life-supporting planet has to be just the right distance from the galactic centre.

There is no point in a planet being in the right place if it does not remain in that area long enough to permit complex life to develop. If its orbit, or the orbit of its system, takes it into areas that are hostile to life, such as an area of high radiation, all life is likely to be extinguished. A planet is more likely to get in harm's way if its orbit is elliptical or hyperbolic. The best galactic orbit is one that is almost circular. Our Solar System orbits the Galactic Centre of the Milky Way in an almost perfect circle and the period of that orbit, happily, matches the rotational period of the galaxy. Luck is on our side again.

As far as we know, water is essential for life, and the water must be in a liquid state, not a solid or gas. Therefore, for a planet to develop complex life, it must be just the right distance from its star so that its water is water, not ice or steam. This is sometimes known as the Goldilocks Principle – the water (porridge) has to be just right. Again, we are lucky, as our Sun, 93 million miles away, is just the right distance from the Earth. We would not want it to be any nearer or further away, or we would end up sizzling like Mercury or freezing like Mars.

Nowadays, there is much talk about global warming and the increase of carbon dioxide (CO_2) in the atmosphere. Earth's atmosphere contains around 390 parts per million of carbon dioxide and, without it, our planet would be about 40 degrees Centigrade cooler than it is. The composition of our atmosphere is just right for us and all the other life forms with which we share this planet, but if we increase the amount of CO_2 or other greenhouse gases in our atmosphere the temperature will rise accordingly, with potentially catastrophic consequences.

For life to emerge and evolve, a rocky planet with certain metals is necessary. The problem is that rocky planets usually form close to their central star, too close for life. Not only must a planet be the right distance from its central star, but the star must be of the right type. One that is too hot will not allow life to develop. In addition, it will probably burn up its energy too quickly for complex life to have time to evolve. Stars, like everything else, are subject to time. After its allotted time, a star will become a Red Giant and subsequently a White Dwarf. This will happen to our Sun, but not for billions of years, as it is now about middle-aged. The Sun will burn up the Earth as a Red Giant before becoming a dying star (White Dwarf). Again, we have been lucky, as our Sun is not of the type that goes through its life cycle so quickly as to be antithetical to complex life. Furthermore, the star has to emit a fixed amount of energy. A sudden increase, or decrease, in output will have disastrous consequences for its neighbouring, life-supporting planets. Our Sun gives out a steady flow of heat. It does go though cycles but none is extreme enough to threaten life. Stars like our Sun are not plentiful in the universe.

For life to develop and evolve, the chemistry must also be just right. Metals are necessary for chemical reactions to take place. They are produced and spread about by supernova explosions. Stars which were formed when the universe was young are low in metals, as are stars on the outer edges of galaxies. Stars which contain the metals deemed necessary for complex life are most likely to be found in a spiral galaxy, which also, coincidentally, will be an area of low radiation. If the central star is metal-poor, then so will its planets be. In such a case, a terrestrial planet will probably not develop. Huge Jovian planets – like our gas giants, Jupiter and Saturn – can condense from a low-metallicity star but, since Jupiter and Saturn do not have hard surfaces, they are not suitable for complex, multicellular life.

Our Solar System is arranged with the Sun in the centre, with small rocky planets next and, beyond them, the gas giants. Earth is in the ideal place. Having Jupiter and Saturn as neighbours, albeit distant ones, is a mixed blessing that balances out. These planets have very strong gravitation and hurl into space bits of planetary debris, left behind after the creation of the Solar System. On the other hand, Earth is often hit with asteroid debris from Jupiter, so it is a case of swings and roundabouts. We do not want Jupiter or Saturn any closer to us, as their proximity could catastrophically affect Earth's orbit. Overall, we do not do too badly and are hit by large chunks only very infrequently. Astronomers are keeping an eye on what is happening with that debris out there, just in case any large potential troublemaker is heading in our direction.

A life-supporting planet needs to be of the right size. If it is too small, it will not be able to retain its atmosphere (like our Moon – which is a satellite, not a planet) and its temperature will be affected. If it is too big, its gravitational force will be very strong, and this will determine the type of life that would develop. They would have to be forms that could withstand huge gravitational force pressing down on them.

Having a large moon nearby is also useful. Of the terrestrial planets in our Solar System, only Earth has a sizeable moon. Mercury and Venus have no satellites, and that of Mars hardly deserves the name, as it is really more like an asteroid. Theia, an object the size of our Moon, is thought to have hit the Earth billions of years ago when the Earth was not fully formed. This became our Moon. The impact of Theia was so intense that it tilted the Earth's axis and increased its speed of rotation. Both these results are beneficial. Our speed of rotation is ideal for photosynthesis. The Earth's tilt is just perfect. Were it any more pronounced, the variation in our seasonal temperatures would be greater, and were it any less, there would be little or no climatic variation – which would not help the development of complex life. Although the Moon's gravity is only one-sixth that of the Earth's, it helps maintain its tilt the way it is.

Without the Moon, tides would be insignificant, as they would be influenced only by the gravitational pull of the distant Sun. The tides have helped with the evolution of life by creating tidepools and 'halfway houses' for life forms in the process of relocating from water to land. We should enjoy and appreciate the Moon while it is still with us. Astronomers tell us that it is slowly breaking away from the Earth's gravitational pull and one day will drift off into space.

If the Rare Earth hypothesis is valid and only time will tell – it would show just how unique and lucky we are to live on such a beautiful, life-friendly planet. It would also show that we have beaten very high odds to be here and, had one of the many variables involved worked out differently, we would probably not be here at all. It the hypothesis is correct, it would also provide an answer to the Fermi paradox – 'If extraterrestrial aliens are common, why aren't they obvious?'

That the Earth contains life is the result of a large number of improbable and fortuitous events. That it contains intelligent life is even more improbable. But, maybe intelligence is overrated! There is a species of box jellyfish – *Tripedalia cystophora* – that, according to marine biologists, has been around for about 150 million years. This jellyfish does not have what could really be called a brain. (It does, however, have 24 eyes!) Yet it has survived, indeed thrived, all those years. The dinosaurs have not been credited with much brainpower, but survived for 165 million years. We have yet to prove ourselves, having been on the planet, in one form or another, for only about three million years. Our big brain has helped us to adapt, to modify (and destroy) our environment and to make life comfortable, at least for the better-off. There are also disadvantages of which the jellyfish would be unaware. Our metabolism is complex, our gestation period longer than that of most mammals, and we are slow to mature, being helpless children, or dependent teenagers, for a large percentage of our lives. We are also unusual in being the only large biped on the planet. (Ostriches or other large avian bipeds do not count here.)

But let's not be too hard on ourselves. We have been gifted with the opposable thumb, which means we are capable of very fine manual dexterity in manipulating objects. With our eyes in the front rather than the side of the head, we have very good hand/eye coordination. Our vocal cords are well developed and can produce a wide range of sounds. Our big brains have developed languages to enable us to use sounds in complex communication, a big advantage in getting ahead as a species. We are capable of engaging in abstract thought, make wonderful discoveries and inventions, develop magical technology and produce sublime music and poetry. To cap it all, we are on the top of the food chain.

When one considers all that has happened since the Big Bang to bring us to where we are now, all the improbable and complex events that have occurred, then we must conclude that we are lucky, very lucky, to be here.

The Placebo Effect

The placebo effect is a well-known phenomenon in medicine and demonstrates how the mind can influence the body. A placebo is a 'sugar' pill or other substance, which is given to some patients or subjects, usually during trials of a new drug. In many cases, patients who are getting the placebo show dramatic improvements in their conditions. The same effect has been observed in 'sham' surgery where the patient is told a certain procedure has been carried out, but in fact, only 'pretend' surgery has been performed.

Coming from the Latin for 'I will please', the effects produced by the placebo (fake) medicine, or surgery, are entirely the result of the patient's belief in the efficacy of the medicine or surgery. A common example is of a patient who complains of pain and is given an injection of, say, sterile water, and soon reports that the pain has gone. The patient believes that a painkilling drug has been administered and the pain disappears.

The effect is likely to be more pronounced in patients who are well informed on their illness and the treatments that they are being given than in patients who are less knowledgeable about their conditions and treatment. One might suspect that the placebo effect occurs because the patients involved are hypochondriacs, who are really not ill, but the effect has even been observed in double-blind tests with seriously-ill people where not only the patient, but also the doctors, do not know who is getting the experimental medicine and who is being given the placebo. In fact, the placebo effect is often regarded as a nuisance that can affect the results and validity of tests.

In cases where patients were given placebos and had shown improvements, but were then informed that the 'medicines' being given were fake, the beneficial effects stopped and the patients' conditions deteriorated. This has raised ethical questions relating to doctors' Hippocratic Oath.

The placebo effect is more common in conditions where the body processes involved are controlled by the brain, such as pain or body temperature. The power of the mind and how it interacts with the body are not fully understood and research continues in this area. The expression 'It's all in the mind' is often used in this context. This implies that the person displaying the placebo effect is either not ill or that the mind has the power to override, or heal, the body. Another medical condition, known as the phantom limb, also shows the complexity of the relationship between mind and body. With the phantom limb, a person who has had a limb amputated occasionally reports feeling pain or other sensation in the missing limb. The mind has not adjusted to the fact that the limb is no longer there.

The placebo effect has sometimes been suggested as a possible reason for the perceived ability of a rabbit's foot, four-leaf clover or any of the other paraphernalia of luck to bring a person good fortune. The possession of such items makes the person 'feel lucky' and if he or she were to win a lottery, or have some other good fortune, they will most likely credit it to the efficacy of their 'lucky' objects. This will further reinforce their belief and they will become even more convinced of the power of these objects. People who do not believe in luck or lucky charms will regard such behaviour as strange, irrational or superstitious. Of course, there is no way to prove that the 'lucky' items caused the good fortune, but neither is there a way to prove that they did not. Most people would agree that a positive mental attitude is more likely to bring success in life than a negative, defeatist mindset. Positive thoughts make a person feel better, more optimistic and more confident of success. Whether or not these feelings increase a person's luck is difficult, perhaps even impossible, to prove. However, a positive approach to life is likely to have benefits for a person, even if they do not cause, or lead to, something like a lottery win. In addition, such a person will react less negatively to bad luck, setbacks or disappointments and will 'bounce back' and keep trying. The negative person, on the other hand, will use every failure as further proof of his bad luck, and sink further into a 'What's the point?' approach to life.

Taking this viewpoint a stage further, it might be contended that a person 'makes' his or her own luck. Maybe it is like the placebo effect – the patient who believes in the medicine or treatment he is receiving (even if it is fake) shows improvement and the person who believes he is lucky will be lucky. If two equally qualified and experienced candidates are interviewed for a position, and one comes across as a positive person while the other appears negative, who is more likely to be offered the job? The positive person will appear more confident, will be a more pleasant colleague and is, consequently, more likely to be a good employee.

If a rabbit's foot or four-leaf clover makes a person feel more confident, then it is at least effective in making them feel more positive. Nothing succeeds like success, and one is more often judged by results than by effort. You could say that it is 'all in the mind', but so is much of life. The world is as we experience and interpret it, not as it is 'in reality'. The only 'reality' we know is what our mind tells us is real. Reality to the hallucinating LSD user is what his drug-affected mind tells him is real, however strange that may be. The furry animals that the hallucinating alcoholic *in delirium tremens* sees coming out of the walls are very real to him, but not to his sober companion.

There is one major difference between belief in luck and the placebo effect. Telling a patient that their 'medicine' is fake has been seen to cause a relapse, but telling a person that their 'lucky' objects are of no use is unlikely to change their beliefs. If it works, why change?

Biorhythm
Biorhythm is an alleged, or hypothetical, cycle of life. According to this hypothesis, intellectual, emotional and physiological processes in the body undergo cycles or rhythms.

Hermann Swoboda, a psychology professor at the University of Vienna, carried out the first work that suggested that biorhythm might exist. He was studying the fluctuations in fevers as well and their frequency. At the same time, he also came up with data on heart attacks, asthma and recurrent dreams. His studies led him to conclude that the body had a 28-day emotional cycle and a 23-day physical cycle.

Without being aware of Swoboda's work, Wilhelm Fliess, an ear and throat specialist, was also studying fevers and recurrent illnesses. His conclusions were exactly the same as those of Swoboda.

Alfred Teltscher, an engineering professor at the University of Innsbruck, calculated the cycles at 33 days, based on his observation of good and bad learning days among his students.

The hypothesis that originated from their work claims that the human body is affected by cycles and that people's behaviour will be impacted, or even determined, by their current biorhythmic state. These states were believed to be related to the body's bioelectricity. Graphs have been drawn up to show the waveforms, which are generally symmetrical. Bioelectric activity was believed to fluctuate, or oscillate, between strong and weak, called positive and negative phases. The rhythm was said to start at birth at its lowest value and then fluctuate between negative and positive, resulting in emotional, physiological and intellectual peaks and troughs. On a person's 58th birthday, approximately, their biorhythm was said to reach once more its lowest level.

Those who accept the hypothesis of biorhythm claim that it is a valid field of scientific study, which is still being developed. Critics, on the other hand, say that it is little more than a kind of numerology. Mathematicians or biologists do not accept its validity. There have been numerous studies on biorhythm which seemed to support its principles, but all have been criticised for containing flaws or errors in either their methodology or their statistical data. At present, it is not accepted among the scientific community.

In the 1970s there was great interest in the matter – particularly, but not only, in the United States. There were even machines, usually in amusement arcades, that were supposed to check one's biorhythm when the date of birth was entered. For those with an interest in the subject, there are internet sites where one can check one's biorhythm.

On a more serious level, some airline and railway companies are known to have taken an interest in biorhythms. There is some anecdotal evidence that people may be more prone to mistakes on days when their biorhythm is said to be down. These are sometimes called 'critical days' and if they do exist it might be useful to know them, so that extra precautions can be taken.

While biologists regard the biorhythm hypothesis as pseudo-science, there is a recognised branch of biology, called chronobiology, which investigates the rhythm of living things. The cycles have been broken down as follows – ultradian (less than 24 hours), circadian (around 24 hours), infradian (a few days), circavigintan (about three weeks), circatrigintan (about a month) and circannual (about a year).

Whether or not the body has a biorhythm, there is no disputing that people have good days and bad days. There are days on which one feels positive, buoyant, optimistic, even lucky, and others on which lethargy, pessimism and negativity seem overpowering. A person's attitudes and behaviour will change with these fluctuations in mood. On a good day one feels lucky to be alive, is alert and visualises a happy future, while on the bad days one is 'down in the dumps' (what Dr Johnson called the 'black dog' of depression) and the future seems to stretch ahead grey, bleak and uninviting. These good or bad days often seem to occur independently of what is happening in a person's life and are not directly caused by good or bad news, or by anything in the external world. Such phrases as 'having the hump' are sometimes used of the bad day, while on a good day one is said to be resident on 'cloud nine' or 'in seventh heaven'. Whether or not these swings are due to a biorhythm is still a matter of debate and one is free to regard the idea of a biorhythm as a valid hypothesis, a bit of fun or an interesting idea.

Lucky/Unlucky people

Frane Selak

We have all met people who moan about their bad luck, complaining that it is the only luck they have. Were they to hear about Frane Selak's run of luck, they might review their opinion. A music teacher from Croatia, Selak has escaped from so many accidents that one is reminded of the saying about the cat with nine lives. While he was unlucky to have had so many accidents, we would have to say he was lucky to escape relatively unscathed. In a way, one might be tempted to say that his good and bad luck evened out, but that somehow does not seem to do him justice. Either way, Selak had a lot of luck.

In January 1962, he was travelling on a train from Sarajevo to Dubrovnik. The train derailed and fell into a river, killing 17 passengers. Selak got away with a broken arm and a few contusions.

In 1963, while flying from Zagreb to Rijeka, the cockpit door suddenly came off. 19 people were killed. Selak landed in a haystack and sustained only minor injuries. Three years later the bus he was travelling on crashed, killing four passengers. Selak was uninjured. In 1970, his car burst into flames due to a defective fuel pump, but he escaped without injury. Three years later, another of his cars caught fire. This time he was not so lucky – most of his hair was burned off. Things went all right for a while after this, but in 1995 he was hit by a bus. The result was minor injuries. The following year he was forced to drive off a cliff to avoid an oncoming truck. He ended up in a tree. His car fell a further 300 feet, and exploded. Seven years later, he won $1,000,000 in the Croatian lottery.

Selak believes that his amazing escapes were because 'God was watching over me'. He admits that he could be called 'the world's unluckiest man or the world's luckiest man'. He prefers to regard himself as the luckiest.

Major Summerford
In February 1918, Major Summerford was doing his duty as a British soldier in Flanders. He was hit by lightning, knocked from his horse and paralysed from the waist down. After retiring from the army, he moved to Vancouver, but the lightning seemed to follow him. In 1924, while fishing from a riverbank, lightning struck a tree, which then fell on him. The result was that he was paralysed down his right side. Summerford fought his paralysis and managed to walk again, but in 1930 he was again struck by lightning. This time he was permanently paralysed. He died in 1932, but lightning was not finished with him yet. Four years after his death, lightning struck the cemetery in which he was buried. One tombstone was destroyed. Guess whose tombstone it was!

Ann Hodges
You have to be pretty unlucky to be struck by a meteorite. Ann Elizabeth Hodges (1923–1972) had such luck. She was relaxing on her living room couch in Sylacauga, Alabama on 30 November 1954, when a meteorite the size of a grapefruit and weighing 8.5 pounds (3.8 kg), crashed through the roof of her house, bounced off her radio and hit her on the hip and arm. She was fortunate (and deserved to be) to escape with only a bruise.

A US Air Force officer arrived to take possession of the meteorite. Feeling that this was not right, Hodges's husband, Eugene, sought legal advice. Their landlord also felt he had a claim on it, as it had damaged his property. At one time, up to $5,000 was offered for the meteorite. Eventually, the Hodges had the meteorite returned to them, but by now, it was no longer a hot topic and could not fetch such a price.

Mrs Hodges was not pleased by the publicity and the unedifying wrangle over ownership. She donated the meteorite to the Alabama Museum of Natural History and it can now be seen at the University of Alabama.

Evelyn Adams
While you have to be unlucky to be struck by a meteorite, you have to be lucky to win the lottery. You have to be twice as lucky to win it twice. Evelyn Adams won the

New Jersey lottery in 1985 and again in 1986. Her total winnings were $5.4 million. 'Everybody wanted my money. Everybody had their hand out,' said Adams. Before long, all the money was gone. She even lost her house. What was not given away was gambled away, as Adams was, by her own description, 'a big-time gambler'.

'I had the American dream,' she said, 'but I lost it. It was a very hard fall.'

In the end, she became philosophical about her situation. 'I made mistakes, some I regret, some I don't. I'm human. I can't go back now, so I just go forward, one step at a time.'

Evelyn Adams was not the only lottery winner who lost it all. In 1983, Suzanne Mullins won $4.2 million in the Virginia lottery. At first, her winnings were paid out in annual cheques, and she had borrowed nearly $200,000 against these payments. When the lottery changed its rules and paid her a lump sum, she neglected to pay back the money she had borrowed. Today she is broke and in debt.

In 1988, William 'Bud' Post won the Pennsylvania lottery. His winnings were $16.2 million. Then his luck changed. First, a former girlfriend sued him. Then his own brother hired a hit man to kill him, but ended up being arrested. He was hounded into investing in the car and restaurant businesses. This relieved him of more of his money. When a bill collector followed him, an exasperated Post fired a pistol over his head and ended up in jail. Within a year, because he was what he called 'careless and foolish' his money was gone and he was $1 million in debt.

'I wish it never happened,' he said. 'It was totally a nightmare.'

Post declared bankruptcy and ended up living on Social Security. Then he suffered heart problems and was operated on for an aneurysm.

'Lotteries don't mean anything to me,' he said shortly before his death from respiratory failure.

John Lyne

John Lyne fell off a horse when he was a child and was then run over by a delivery van. This was the start of a long series of accidents. In his teens, he fell from a tree and broke his arm. After being treated in hospital, he took the bus home. The bus crashed and he broke the same arm, in another place. Known as 'Calamity John', he has been struck by lightning, was involved in three car accidents and was injured in a mine rock fall, to mention but a few. He has been involved in a total of sixteen accidents.

'I don't think there is any reason or explanation,' he said. 'Things could have been much worse and I could have died, but it doesn't worry me too much.'

Polycrates and Amasis

In Book III of *The Histories* by Herodotus, we read of Polycrates, the son of Aeaces, who controlled Samos. On the death of Aeaces, control of the state was divided between his three sons. This was not to Polycrates' liking, so he killed one of his brothers, Pantagnotus, and banished the other, Syloson. After this, he ruled the island alone and before long had built up a large fleet.

According to Herodotus, 'Herewith he plundered all, without distinction of friend or foe; for he argued that a friend was better pleased if you gave back what you had taken from him, than if you spared him at the first.' Polycrates was successful in everything he attempted and before long his fame had spread through all Greece. It had even reached as far as Egypt and its king, Amasis. The two rulers exchanged correspondence and presents. However, Amasis was disturbed by the constant success of Polycrates and sent the following letter to Samos.

> Amasis to Polycrates thus sayeth: It is a pleasure to hear of a friend and ally prospering, but thy exceeding prosperity does not cause me joy, forasmuch as I know that the gods are envious. My wish for myself and for those whom I love is to be now successful, and now to meet with a check; thus passing through life amid alternate good and ill, rather than with perpetual good fortune. For never yet did I hear tell of any one succeeding in all his undertakings, who did not meet with calamity at last, and come to utter ruin. Now, therefore, give ear to my words, and meet thy good luck in this way: bethink thee which of all thy treasures thou valuest most and canst least bear to part with; take it, whatever it may be, and throw it away, so thwart it may be sure never to come any more into the sight of man. Then, if thy good fortune be not thenceforth chequered with ill, save thyself from harm by again doing as I have counselled.

(Translation by George Rawlinson)

When Polycrates received this letter, he considered it carefully and decided to do as the king had advised. He thought a lot about what he should throw away and eventually decided on an emeraldand-gold signet ring. He got on a boat and, when he had travelled a long distance from the island, threw the treasured ring into the sea.

A few days later, a fisherman caught a fish that was so big and beautiful that he decided to take it to Polycrates as a gift. Polycrates thanked the man for the fish and invited him to have supper with him. The fish was sent to the kitchen to be cleaned and cooked. As soon as the fish was cut open, the first thing the servant saw was her master's signet ring. The ring was returned to Polycrates, who 'saw something providential in the matter' and decided to write to Amasis, telling him everything that had happened.

When Amasis had read the letter… he perceived that it does not belong to man to save his fellow-man from the fate which is in store for him; likewise he felt certain that Polycrates would end ill, as he prospered in everything, even finding what he had thrown away. So he sent a herald to Samos, and dissolved the contract of friendship. This he did, that when the great and heavy misfortune came, he might escape the grief which he would have felt if the sufferer had been his bond-friend.

Polycrates continued to prosper for many more years, but his conquests had made many enemies and his success aroused envy. Oroetes, the governor of Sardis, was particularly displeased by his good fortune. Oroetes was very eager to bring Samos under the control of the Persian Empire. He invited Polycrates to Sardis and had him assassinated. Herodotus does not tell us how Polycrates was killed, but it is thought that he was impaled and then crucified.

Chapter 8

Luck: How to Improve It

Luck has a peculiar habit of favouring those who don't depend on it.
Anon

Some folk want their luck buttered.
Thomas Hardy

The wind and waves are always on the side of the ablest navigators.
Edward Gibbon

Be ready when opportunity comes. Luck is the time when preparation and opportunity meet.
Roy D Chapin Jr

Good luck is another name for tenacity of purpose.
Ralph Waldo Emerson

The harder I work, the luckier I get.
Sam Goldwyn

> *Go and wake up your luck.*
> Persian saying

If you look through a selection of quotations on luck, you will find everything from 'Luck is everything' to 'There is no such thing as luck'. For those who do not believe in luck, the question of trying to improve it is not an issue. For the hundreds of millions who do, the possibility of improving it sounds enticing.

People who have a strong belief in luck will be careful to court 'lady luck'. For such people there is no shortage of objects they can utilise in attempting to improve their luck. There are the oft-mentioned old reliables like rabbits' feet, four-leaf clovers, horseshoes etc. There are fortune-tellers, astrologers, psychic hotlines and a host of other methods. A look through the Internet will reveal all sorts of methods that promise to improve one's luck – talismans, 'lucky' numbers, mantras, winning formulas and a host of others. If such things help, or are believed to help, improve luck, then it would seem to be sensible to use them. While it would not be possible to prove that such things bring good fortune, it would be equally impossible to prove that they do not.

Those who do not accept the existence of luck will brand believers as superstitious losers who do not have the intelligence or common sense to know that their fate is in their own hands and has nothing to do with luck. Such views are unlikely to have much effect on believers. And the fact of the matter is that it is not just losers or 'cop-outs' who believe in luck. Many of the rich and famous, as noted earlier, are known to believe in luck or 'lucky' objects, and it is not unusual to hear a celebrity express thanks for his or her good fortune.

Even if one believes the universe is deterministic and that fate plays a significant role in people's lives, it is very unlikely that an individual will improve his luck by giving into destiny completely and becoming fatalistic. There is no doubt that people do not have full control over their lives, but it would be equally fallacious to believe that they have none. While a person may not be in control of everything that happens to him, he is in control of how he reacts to what happens to him, and what he subsequently does. Good and bad things happen to everyone. There is disappointment, ill health, bereavement, poverty and ultimately death. But there is also love, joy, success, reward and hope. How a person reacts to those things will, in large part, determine the quality of his life. 'Making the best of things' and accepting the bad with dignity and resignation, while trying to move on and to do one's best, is obviously preferable to wallowing in the bad and allowing it to poison every aspect of life. The power of positive thinking is well known. So is the power of negative thinking. The positive person is ready when opportunity knocks, but those who are negative are more likely to complain about the disturbance.

William James said that you could change your life by changing the way you think. Mark McCormick advised 'Don't mix with losers'. 'Misery loves company', the proverb goes, and regular association with negative people is likely to pull one down. Such 'psychic vampires' suck the positivity from a person and can reduce him to their own level. On the other hand, positive people who have learned to make the best of things and are alert for opportunities make convivial and encouraging company. Nothing succeeds like success.

Studies on what makes people happy have revealed some surprising results. The things that many believe are recipes for happiness, such as money and good looks, do not often rate highly in such studies. In fact, feeling useful, wanted and appreciated seem to be the most important factors.

Looked at from a biological viewpoint, it seems that the main reason why some people are happy and others not is down to genetics. There are people whom we think should be happy or unhappy, but in fact are the opposite. One seems to be born happy or unhappy. Some would say that it is the same with luck – you are born with it or without it. This has given rise to the saying, 'It is better to be born lucky than rich'.

Were life a level playing field, were people given wealth, health, talent and opportunities equally, there would be no need, or excuse, for luck. Sadly, life is not like that. Some are dealt better hands than others (by the Fates?). A person is stuck with the hand he is dealt and must play it as best he can. The only other choice is to throw in one's hand.

When learning about successful people, almost invariably one finds that there was a time in their lives when they took a major chance. Being willing to take a calculated risk, as long as it is not reckless or foolhardy, is often an opportunity to turn life around for the better. Of course, it can also work the other way, when the risk does not pay off. Successful people are not always successful and the occasional loss or bad decision is part of their lives. They do not sit around afterwards complaining about it, but will move on and learn from the experience. Some people who are in a rut, or who lead monotonous lives, have the idea that if they wait long enough, something will happen to change (hopefully improve) their lives – something will 'turn up'. They are right. One thing a person can be sure of in life is change. Even if they do nothing deliberate or definite to change their lives, time moves on, the world changes and their time becomes shorter.

Some sit around bemoaning their luck and comparing themselves enviously to others, who they believe have been treated more generously by Fate. When it comes to comparison, it all depends on what is being compared. Let us take two tennis players, A and B. They are friends and colleagues, but as soon as they hit the tennis court, this is forgotten and they become fiercely competitive. On the occasion in question, let's say that A beats B soundly. A feels very good about this. B does not feel quite so good. On the drive home, A congratulates himself on his victory. He tells himself he is a fine tennis player. A warm glow rises within him and he is happy. However, happiness is fickle and transitory. Another thought comes to mind. He thinks, 'B is not a very good player. So, beating him is not much of an achievement.' He sinks further – 'What if I were to play a professional? Then I'd look pretty poor.' He continues to sink. Now he is convinced he is a very bad player. He manages to level out, and struggles upwards, looking for a comfort zone. Hope springs eternal. 'What if I were to buy some really good tennis equipment, join a top-notch club and take lessons? Then I would become a really good player.' This thought makes him more positive. He can buy success and happiness. Why not? Any time A turns on the television or looks on the Internet, there are advertisements telling him just that – buy a new car and be happy, go on an exotic holiday, use Brand X washing powder, use Brand Y aftershave, drink Brand Z alcohol, get a bigger house and a bigger mortgage – and be happy. Happiness is just another commodity, to be bought and sold like coffee or pork bellies. Could it be the same with luck? Can you buy that too?

A was happy while comparing downwards to B, but then lost that happiness when he compared upwards to tennis professionals. No one is suggesting that a person look down on another. A should just have enjoyed his tennis win without any comparisons, but it is in the nature of man, and society, to compare and to rate. He should have been satisfied with what he had. The proverb 'I complained because I had no shoes, until I met a man who had no legs' is a graphic way of expressing the same idea.

In Buddhism, desire is one of the main causes of unhappiness and ties people to their lives. This is not a very popular idea in this age of conspicuous consumption and instant gratification. For ordinary mortals, it is hard to resist the desire for more and, if only you were luckier – or richer – you tell yourself, you would be happy. Maybe not. There will always be something you want that you cannot have, and there are things that money cannot buy. Some people seem to have a capacity for happiness, while others do not. It seems to be the same with luck.

But how lucky or unlucky are you? The answer you give to this question is likely to be very subjective. Others, looking from the outside, may take a different view. So is there any way that one can *objectively* determine how lucky or unlucky one is? Maslow's hierarchy of needs provides a useful guideline for anyone trying to decide how well or badly off they are. A person can find his position in the hierarchy and then decide how fortunate or unfortunate he is.

Maslow's Hierarchy of Needs

In his 1943 *A Theory of Human Motivation,* Abraham H Maslow studied the lives of what he called 'exemplary people', such as Eleanor Roosevelt and Albert Einstein, rather than 'crippled, stunted, immature and unhealthy specimens' in an effort to determine, among other things, what makes up quality of life.

Maslow came up with a hierarchy of a person's need, ranking them in order of importance. These needs are often represented as a pyramid. The pyramid has five levels. Physiological needs are situated at the base of the pyramid, as they are the most basic, while on the top he placed what he called 'self-actualisation'. Physiological needs include those that are necessary for human survival. Breathing, water, food, sleep, excretion, shelter, clothing and sex would be included here. Moving up the pyramid, we next come to what could be called 'safety' needs. Once a person has procured the basics, he looks for things such as justice, work, money and protection from political persecution, or unjust government. He wants personal and financial security, and assistance when in bad health or dire straits.

Next on the pyramid are 'social' needs. The Bible says that it is not good for man to be alone, and most would agree that humans are social (some might say herd) animals. Having healthy and supportive relationships, friendship and a feeling that one is a welcome member of a group, are important to most people. This is the main reason people join clubs and organisations. These groups can be a gang, a club, a sports team, a religious group or a support group. People want to be loved and to have satisfying social interactions – they want partners, friends, colleagues and confidants, in order to avoid loneliness, isolation and depression. They want to 'belong'.

People also crave esteem, the next level on the pyramid. They want respect and a feeling of being valued. They crave acceptance and recognition of their perceived worth. This can even extend to the desire, or need, for fame – even glory. Deprived of those things, most will tend to experience low self-esteem or feelings of inferiority, which may lead to psychological problems.

On the apex of the pyramid are aesthetic needs or 'self–actualisation'. Here, a person wants to achieve his full potential, to 'be the best he can be'. According to Maslow's earlier hierarchy, this is the final need. It seems as if things don't get better than that. But later in life, Maslow added another level to the top of the hierarchy. This level could be called 'self-transcendence'. In *Transpersonal Psychology and Self-Transference*, he wrote of such people as 'being much more aware of the realm of Being' and 'to have peak experience (mystic, sacral, ecstatic) with illuminations and insights'. These are clearly superior people who have reached a very elevated and refined level of living. Maslow estimated that no more than 2% of the population will ever reach this standard. These are the great humanitarians. They will strive to help others and delight in the success of family members, colleagues, friends and people in general. They think of the good of their fellow man rather than their own pleasure or satisfaction.

A person can determine his or her level on the pyramid and then decide how fortunate or unfortunate they are. Those who never reach above the most basic level (a large percentage of the world's population) would be justified in considering themselves unlucky to find they are so poorly endowed with the good things of life. Even if their condition is brought about partly or mainly by their own actions or omissions, we will sympathise with their situation. Often their situation will be so abject that there is no way they can reach a higher level. There will, of course, be some who have 'brought it on themselves', but for most it will be a condition into which they were born, and from which they are unable to escape. Those who have achieved the second level can count themselves more fortunate and their lives will not be a constant struggle to obtain the basics necessary for existence. They will have more pleasure in living and are more likely to be happy, or at least contented. Those on level three do not have to worry too much about the basics and have the time and means to concentrate on more elevated things. The truly lucky are those who have reached the highest level, where they can concentrate on nobler things than worrying where their next meal will come from or where they will sleep that night. They have reached their full potential, whether by luck or hard work or a combination of both, and can now look outside themselves and try to improve the conditions of their fellow man.

Nowadays, science and technology are held in high esteem, and so they should be. There is no disputing the fact that they have given us many wonderful things that have made life easier, safer, longer and healthier. Science and technology are the future. In some ways, in the minds of many the gods of religion have been replaced by the principles of science. Now we want scientific proof for everything and, if that proof is not forthcoming, then the matter in question is usually relegated to the realm of the fake and is ignored. Miracles, astrology and the paranormal fall within this category. There is no 'proof' and therefore they do not exist. They are dismissed as superstition, or the product of pre-logical thinking. It is not being suggested that we should go back to the Dark Ages, but keeping an open mind is one of the prerequisites of a valid science. Scientists are still looking for a Unified Field Theory, and who knows what they will find.

In general, scientists are very sceptical – or, more probably, dismissive – of luck. Despite the contributions made by serendipity and intuition, such scepticism can be understood and must be respected. One problem is that luck is not the type of thing that can be hauled into a laboratory and subjected to a battery of tests. Luck is not seen as a suitable subject for study. Despite this, it may be possible to subject one aspect of luck to the rigours of scientific method, in the hope that it might cast a little light on this translucent area.

Let's look again at gambling luck, and particularly in games where randomness plays a significant part, such as roulette. While this experiment may not reveal much about luck, or even randomness, it might be of interest, and one does not want to pre-empt the outcome by deciding in advance what that outcome might be.

For this experiment, we will select five players and sit them down at a roulette table. Player A is a firm believer in luck. He has been careful, in the preceding days, not to do any of the things that are generally regarded as bringing bad luck. He has also taken the precaution of bringing to the table a rabbit's foot, a four-leaf clover and some other items which, he believes, will enhance his luck. Player B is the opposite of A. He does not believe in luck, good or bad. In fact, he is contemptuous of the whole idea of luck. Before the experiment, he has walked under numerous ladders, opened and closed umbrellas indoors countless times, set out to find black cats, broken mirrors and put shoes on tables and beds. Player C is neutral. He has no strong belief in luck, one way or the other. He approaches the game as a gamble and will not blame luck if he loses, or credit it if he wins. Player D plays blindfolded, placing his chips on the board wherever his hand happens to stop. Player E is above it all, whether good luck, bad luck or randomness, because he has a 'system'.

The five subjects will play roulette for twelve hours, or until their money runs out, whichever comes first. Each is given 10,000 credits and must bet 20 credits on each turn of the wheel. They may bet on individual numbers, groups of numbers, colours, odd/even, or whatever they wish. If a player loses all his chips, he is out of the game. At the end of the twelve hours, the chips of each player are counted and the winner is the one with the most credits.

While the experiment might be interesting, it would not produce any scientifically valid results. Science likes experiments that can be repeated indefinitely, ideally with the same outcome, thus amounting to proof. With our experiment, a repetition would be unlikely to produce a similar result. What is likely to be proved would be randomness and unpredictability. In addition, luck – at least short-term luck – is also likely to be a feature, and it would not be surprising to see 'runs' of good or bad luck. Even if a player has appeared to have had a run of luck, either good or bad, this would probably have balanced out over a period of time, though it would be difficult or impossible to predict how long a period that would be.

Not only would science be unlikely to accept the results, but the players (at least the losers) would probably argue over the outcome, too. Player A, while still believing in luck, might complain that his luck was 'out' and that he would need longer than twelve hours for his luck to have a fair chance. Player D would likely complain that he would have played better had he not been blindfolded. Player E, still believing in his 'system', would probably ask for more time and a repeat of the experiment. It is like that with luck. Each person has his own belief, and even if circumstances do not lend support to that belief, it is unlikely to change. People buy lottery tickets for years without winning. They still hope to win, and they cannot win if they do not have a ticket. So they buy another ticket. Indeed, the longer they go without winning, the more likely they are to feel they will be lucky, as they are 'due' a win. Of course they are, according to probability, and will have a win eventually, but when or how much is impossible to say.

As alluded to earlier, research has shown that people can become addicted to their beliefs and opinions in the same way that one can become addicted to heroin, alcohol or nicotine. If they are forced to abandon long-held and cherished beliefs, they will show withdrawal symptoms and intermittent urges to go back to those beliefs.

If nothing else seems to work, there is always *amor fati* ('love of fate'). In *The Genealogy of Morals*, the German philosopher Friedrich Nietzsche wrote, 'My formula for greatness in a human being is *amor fati*, that one wants nothing to be different, not forward, not backwards, not in all eternity. Not merely to bear what is necessary, still less conceal it – but love it.'

Those who accept *amor fati* believe that everything that happens is destiny, and should be accepted as good. *Amor fati* is very similar to *Gam Zu Letova*, the Jewish belief that, no matter what happens, 'This too is for the best'.

Knowing something of the history of belief in luck, randomness, cause-and-effect, odds and determinism puts a person in a stronger position to assess, objectively, the phenomenon of luck, even though it is unlikely to change their belief or lack of belief. Perhaps it is our Fate to be so.

Good luck!

References and Further Reading

Chapter 1 Luck – Fact or Fiction

Nagel, Thomas. 'Moral Luck' in *Mortal Questions*. Cambridge: Cambridge University Press, 1979.

Williams, Bernard. 'Moral Luck' in *Moral Luck*. Cambridge: Cambridge University Press, 1981.

Wolf, Susan R. *Freedom Within Reason*. Oxford: Oxford University Press, 1990.

––. 'Moral Saints'. *The Journal of Philosophy*, 79:8 (August 1982), 419–439.

Internet references

'Destiny and Free Will'. www.akgupta.com/Thoughts/destiny.htm

Dictionary of the History of Ideas http://xtf.lib.virginia.edu/xtf/view?docId=DicHist/uvaBook/tei/DicHist1.xml

'What is Destiny?' www.members.tripod.com/tathagata2000/destiny.htm

Chapter 2 Luck and Cause and Effect

Aristotle. *Metaphysics*, Book V, Part 1.

––. *Posterior Analytics*, Book II, Part 2.

Frede, Michael. 'The Original Notion of Cause' in Schofield, Malcolm, Myles Burnyeat and Jonathan Barnes (eds.), *Doubt and Dogmatism: Studies in Hellenistic Epistemology*. Oxford: Oxford University Press, 1980.

Hankinson, R.J. *Cause and Explanation in Ancient Greek Thought*. Oxford: Clarendon Press, 1998.

Hilborn, Robert C. 'Sea Gulls, Butterflies and Grasshoppers: A Brief History of the Butterfly Effect in Nonlinear Dynamics'. *American Journal of Physics*, 72 (2004), 425–427.

Honderich, Ted. *How Free Are You? The Determinism Problem*. Oxford: Oxford University Press, 1993.

Russell, Bertrand. *Human Knowledge*. Simon and Schuster, 1948.

Spirtes, Peter, Clark Glymour and Richard Scheines. *Causation, Prediction and Search*. Cambridge, MA: MIT Press, 1993.

Strohman, Richard C. (2003). 'Genetic Determinism as a Failing Paradigm in Biology and Medicine: Implications for Health and Wellness'. *Journal of Social Work Education*, 39:2 (Spring–Summer 2003).

Van Inwagen, Peter. *An essay on Free Will*. Oxford: Clarendon Press, 1983.

Woodward, James. *Making Things Happen: A Theory of Causal Explanation*. New York: Oxford University Press, 2003.

Internet references

'Fatalism' in Stanford Encyclopedia of Philosophy http://plato.stanford.edu/entries/fatalism

'Fatalism vs. Free Will' in *Project Worldview* www.projectworldview.org/wvtheme11.htm

'Free Will' in Stanford Encyclopedia of Philosophy http//plato.stanford.edu/entries/freewill

'Processes and Causality'. www.jfsowa.com/ontology/causal.htm

'The Butterfly Effect – Variations on a Meme'. http://blog.ap42.com/2011/08/03/the-butterfly-effect-variations-on-a-meme/

Chapter 3 Magic and Luck

Bartlett, Robert. *Trial by Fire and Water: The Mediaeval Judicial Ordeal*. New York: Clarendon Press, 1986.

de Givry, Grillot. *Witchcraft, Magic and Alchemy*. Trans. J. Courtenay Locke, 1931.

Frazer, Sir James George. *Taboo and the Perils of the Soul*. Vol. 3 of *The Golden Bough* (3rd ed.). London: Macmillan and Co. Limited, 1911.

––. *The Magic Art and the Evolution of Kings*. Vols. 1 and 2 of *The Golden* Bough (3rd ed.). London: Macmillan and Co. Limited, 1911.

Holden, Lynn. *Enclyclopedia of Taboos*. Oxford : ABC-CLIO Ltd., 2000.

Thomas, N. W. 'Magic' in *Encyclopædia Britannica*, 11th ed. (1910–11) Vol. 26: 337.

Thorndike, Lynn. *A History of Magic and Experimental Science*. 8 vols. New York: Macmillan, 1923–58.

Vold, George B., Thomas J. Bernard and Jeffrey B. Snipes. *Theoretical Criminology*. New York: Oxford University Press, 2001.

Internet references

'Medieval Sourcebook: Ordeal of Boiling Water, 12th or 13th century'. www.fordham.edu/halsall/source/water-ordeal.html

'Ordeals' in *The Catholic Encyclopedia*. New York: Robert Appleton Company, 1913. Article available at www.newadvent.org/cathen/11276b.htm

Chapter 4 Philosophy, Religion and Luck

Aquinas, Thomas. *Summa Theologica*.

Becker, Lawrence C. *A New Stoicism*. Princeton, NJ: Princeton University Press, 1999.

Boettner, Loraine. *Reformed Doctrine of Predestination*. 1932. Available at www.ccel.org/ccel/boettner/predest.html

Boyd, Gregory A. *God of the Possible*. Ada, MI: Baker Books, 2000.

Braaten, Carl E., *Principles of Lutheran Theology*. Philadelphia, PA: Fortress Press, 1983. (ELCA perspective)

Calvin, John. *Institutes of the Christian Religion* Ed. John T. McNeill, trans. Ford L. Battles. Louisville, KY: Westminster John Knox Press, 1960.

Edwards, Paul. *Reincarnation: A Critical Examination*. Amherst, NY: Prometheus Books, 2001.

Fisher, George Park. *History of Christian Doctrine*. Edinburgh: T&T Clark, 1997.

Kearley, F. Furman. *The Biblical Doctrine of Predestination, Foreordination, and Election*. www.apologeticspress.org/rr/reprints/Biblical-Doctrine-of-Predestina.pdf.

Lange, Lyle W. *God So Loved the World: A Study of Christian Doctrine*. Milwaukee, WI: Northwestern Publishing House, 2006. (WELS perspective)

Long, A. A. and D. N. Sedley. *The Hellenistic Philosophers* (2 vols.). Cambridge: Cambridge University Press, 1987.

Marcus Aurelius. *Meditations*. Trans. Maxwell Staniforth (London: Penguin 60s, 1995) or Gregory Hays (London: Phoenix, 2003).

Oates, Whitney Jenning (ed.). *The Stoic and Epicurean Philosophers: The Complete Extant Writings of Epicurus, Epictetus, Lucretius and Marcus Aurelius*. New York: Random House (9th printing), 1940.

Ryrie, Charles C. *Balancing the Christian Life*. Chicago, IL: Moody Publishers, 1994.

Stevenson, Ian. *Children Who Remember Previous Lives: A Question of Reincarnation*. Revised edition. Jefferson, NC: McFarland, 2001.

—. *Twenty Cases Suggestive of Reincarnation.* 2nd (revised and enlarged) ed. Charlottesville, VA: University of Virginia Press, 1988.

Strange, K. Steven and Jack Zupko (eds.). *Stoicism: Traditions and Transformations.* Cambridge: Cambridge University Press, 2004.

Westminster Confession of Faith (1646), Ch. 3.

Internet references

Boice, James Montgomery. 'God's Providence'.

www.the-highway.com/providence_Boice.html

'Determinism in Theology: Predestination' in *The Dictionary of the History of Ideas.* http://xtf.lib.virginia.edu/xtf/view?docId=DicHist/uvaBook/tei/DicHist1.xml

'Divine Providence' in *The Catholic Encyclopedia.* Article available at www.newadvent.org/cathen/12510a.htm

'Luck in the Bible and Various Minutiae'. Blog published by Smijer on 30 January 2009. http://tete-tete-tete.com/801/luck-in-the-bible-and-various-minutiae/

'Understanding Predestination in Islam'. www.ahya.org/amm/modules.php?name=Sections&op=view article&artid-12

'What does the Bible say about luck?' http://www.gotquestions.org/luck.html

Chapter 5 Probability and Luck

Alexander, J. McKenzie. 'Evolutionary Game Theory' in *The Stanford Encyclopedia of Philosophy* (Fall 2009). http://plato.stanford.edu/entries/game-evolutionary/

Bennett, Deborah J. *Randomness.* Cambridge, MA: Harvard University Press, 1998.

Bloch, Arthur. *Murphy's Law, and Other Reasons Why Things Go Wrong.* Los Angeles, CA: Price/Stern/Sloane Publishers, Inc., 1980.

Bridgman, P. W. *The Logic of Modern Physics.* Reprint: Macmillan, 1927.

Briggs, John and F. David Peat. *Turbulent Mirror: An Illustrated Guide to Chaos Theory and the Science of Wholeness.* New York: Harper Perennial, 1990.

Chaitin, Gregory J. *Exploring Randomness.* London: Springer-Verlag, 2001.

Feller, William. *An Introduction to Probability Theory and Its Applications.* 2 vols. Wiley, 1957.

Gibbons, Robert. *Game theory for Applied Economics.* Princeton, NJ: Princeton University

Press, 1999. Published in Europe as *A Primer in Game Theory* (London: Harvester Wheatsheaf, 1992).

Gleick, James. *Chaos: Making a New Science*. New York: Penguin, 1988.

Hartman, Charles O. *Virtual Muse: Experiments in Computer Poetry*. Hanover, NH: Wesleyan University Press, 1996.

Holt, Alfred. 'Review of the Progress of Steam Shipping during the last Quarter of a Century'. *Minutes of Proceedings of the Institution of Civil Engineers*, Vol. LI, Session 1877–78 Part 1 at 2.8 (Session of 13 November 1877). London: Institution of Civil Engineers, 1878.

Jaynes, Edwin Thomson. *Probability Theory: The Logic of Science*. St Louis, MO: Washington University, 1996.

Jeffrey, Richard. *Probability and the Art of Judgment*. Cambridge: Cambridge University Press, 1992.

Lorenz, Edward N. *The Essence of Chaos*. Seattle, WA: University of Washington Press, 1996.

Maskelyne, Nevil. 'The Art In Magic'. *The Magic Circular,* June 1908, 25.

Osborne, Martin J. *An Introduction to Game Theory*. USA: Oxford University Press, 2004.

Poundston, William. *Prisoner's Dilemma: John von Neumann, Game Theory and the Puzzle of the Bomb*. London: Anchor, 1993.

Ross, Don. 'Game Theory' in *The Stanford Encyclopedia of Philosophy* (Spring 2008). Edward N. Zelda (ed). http://plato.stanford.edu/archives/win2012/entries/game-theory/

Russell, Bertrand. *Human Knowledge*. New York: Simon and Schuster, 1948.

Sneyers, Raymond. 'Climate Chaotic Instability: Statistical Determination and Theoretical Background'. *Environmetrics*, 8:5 (September-October 1997), 517–532.

Stewart, Ian. *Does God Play Dice?: The New Mathematics of Chaos*. Oxford: Blackwell, 1999.

Taleb, Nassim Nicholas. *Fooled by Randomness*. 2nd ed. USA: Thomson Texere, 2004.

UK Gambling Commission

US Gaming Law

Venn, John. *The Logic of Chance*. London: Macmillan, 1866.

Waldrop, M. Mitchell. *Complexity: The Emerging Science at the Edge of Order and Chaos*. New York: Simon and Shuster, 1992.

Internet references

'Different Odds Display Styles' www.free-bets-guide.com/articles/Different%2bOdds%2bDisplay%2bStyles/index.html

Levine, David K. 'What is Game Theory?' Department of Economics, UCLA. http://levine.sscnet.ucla.edu/general/whatis.htm

Office of Public Sector Information (UK): Definition of 'Gaming'. www.legislation.gov.uk/all?title=definition%20of%20gaming

'Probability' in University of Glasgow Statistics Glossary by Easton, Valerie. J and John H. McColl. www.stats.gla.ac.uk/steps/glossary/probability.html

Probability Theory. www.probabilitytheory.info/content/item/7-monkeys-typing-shakespeare-or-even-just-the-word-hamlet

'*Six Reels of Film to Be Shown in Any Order* (1971)'. BFI Film and TV Database. http://ftvdb.bfi.org.uk/sift/title/50946

'*SN*, a film by Fred Camper', (2002). www.fredcamper.com/F/SN.html

The Man Who Broke the Bank at Monte Carlo (1935) at the Internet Movie Database. www.imdb.com

The Man Who Broke the Bank at Monte Carlo: A Music Hall Song, written and composed by Fred Gilbert, sung by Charles Coburn. *Traditional British Songs, Popular Songs of England and Scotland and Wales* at www.know-britain.com

Chapter 6 Luck and Coincidence

Besant, Annie and Charles W. Leadbeater. *Man: How, Whence, and Whither?* (1947). Available at https://archive.org/details/manwhencehowandw031919mbp

Bruce, Martin. 'Coincidences: Remarkable or Random'. *Skeptical Inquirer*, 22:5 (September/October 1998). www.csicop.org/si/show/coincidences_remarkable_or_random/

Capra, Fritjof. *The Web of Life.* London: Harper Collins, 1996.

Carroll, Lewis. *Through the Looking-Glass.* Ch. 5, 'Wool and Water'.

Chopra, Deepak. *How to Know God.* London: Rider Books, 2000.

Clarke, Arthur C. *The View from Serendip.* New York: Random House, 1977.

Eldredge, Niles. *The Pattern of Evolution.* New York: W. H. Freeman & Co., 1999.

Elkins, Don, James Allen McCarty and Carla Rueckert. *The Ra Material: An Ancient Astronaut Speaks.* Virginia Beach, VA: The Donning Company, 1984.

Gallo, Ernest. 'Synchronicity and the Archetypes'. *Skeptical Inquirer*, 18:4 (Summer 1994).

Gibbons, Ann. 'Human Ancestors Were an Endangered Species'. *Science Now*, 19 January 2010. Available online at http://news.sciencemag.org/2010/01/human-ancestors-were-endangered-species

––. *The First Humans: The Race to Discover our Earliest Ancestors.* USA: Anchor Books, 2007.

Havil, Julian. *Nonplussed!: Mathematical Proof of Implausible Ideas.* Princeton, NJ: Princeton University Press, 2007.

Jung, Carl J. *Jung on Synchronicity and the Paranormal.* London: Routledge, 1997.

––. *Synchronicity: An Acausal Connecting Principle.* Princeton, NJ: Princeton University Press, 1973.

––. *The Development of Personality.*

Koestler, Arthur. *The Roots of Coincidence.* New York: Random House, 1973.

Lundstrom, Meg. 'A Wink from the Cosmos'. *Intuition Magazine,* May 1996. Available at www.flowpower.com/What%20is%20Synchronicity.htm

Main, Roderick. 'Religion, Science and Synchronicity'. *Harvest: Journal for Jungian Studies,* 46:2 (2000), 89–107.

Marks, David. *The Psychology of the Psychic.* Amherst, NY: Prometheus Books, 1994.

Myers, David G. 'The Power of Coincidence'. *E-Skeptic,* 23 September 2002. Available at www.davidmyers.org/coincidence

Rampino, Michael. 'Bottleneck in human evolution and the Toba eruption'. *Science,* 262:5142 (24 December 1993), 1955.

Remer, Theodore G. (ed.) *Serendipity and the Three Princes, from the* Peregrinaggio *of 1557.* Norman, OK: University of Oklahoma Press, 1965.

Roberts, Royston M. *Serendipity: Accidental Discoveries in Science.* Hoboken, NJ: Wiley, 1989.

Sugrue, Thomas. *There is a River: The Story of Edgar Cayce.* New York: Dell Publishing, 1974.

Van Andel, Pek. 'Anatomy of the unsought finding. Serendipity: Origin, history, domains, traditions, appearances, patterns and programmability'. *British Journal for the Philosophy of Science,* 45:2 (1994), 631–648.

Yeats, William Butler. *A Vision.* New York: Scribner, 1935.

Internet references

'20 Most Amazing Coincidences' in Oddee: A Blog on the Oddities of Our World. http://oddee.com/item_82923.aspx

'Akashic record' in *The Skeptic's Dictionary.* www.skepdic.com/akashic.html

'Coincidence'. http://www.cut-the-knot.org/do_you_know/coincidence.shtml

'Synchronicity' in *The Skeptic's Dictionary.* www.skepdic.com/jung.html

Unlikely Events – and Coincidence www.csj.org/infoserv_articles/astop_unlikely_events.htm

Chapter 7 Luck and Related Phenomena

Aeschylus. *Agamemnon*.

Barrow, John D. *The Origins of the Universe: To the Edge of Space and Time*. London: Phoenix Books, 1994.

–– and Frank J. Tipler. *The Anthropic Cosmological Principle*. Oxford: Oxford University Press, 1986.

Bender, Tom. *Building with the Breath of Life: Working with Chi Energy in Our Homes and Communities*. Nehalem, OR: Fire River Press, 2000.

Broad, William J. *The Oracle: The Lost Secrets and Hidden Message of Ancient Delphi*. New York: Penguin Press, 2006.

Brown, Colin. *Miracles and the Critical Mind*. Grand Rapids, MI: Eerdmans, 1984.

Bruun, Ole. *An Introduction to Feng Shui*. Cambridge: Cambridge University Press, 2008.

Cairns, Douglas L. '*Hybris*, Dishonour, and Thinking Big.' *Journal of Hellenic Studies*, 116 (November 1996), 1–32.

Chambers' Cyclopaedia (1728).

Curnow, T. *The Oracles of the Ancient World: A Comprehensive Guide*. London: Duckworth, 1995.

Davies, Paul. *The Mind of God: Science and the Search for Ultimate Meaning*. London: Simon and Schuster, 1992.

De Marchi, John. *The True Story of Fatima*. St Paul, MN: Catechetical Guild Educational Society, 1956.

Drayer, Ruth. *Numerology: The Power in Numbers – A Right and Left Brain Approach*. 3rd ed., revised. Portland, OR: Jewels of Light Publishing, 2002.

Dudley, Underwood. *Numerology: Or, What Pythagoras Wrought*. Washington, DC: Mathematical Association of America, 1997.

Einstein, Albert. 'Space-Time' in *Encyclopædia Britannica*, 13th ed. (1911).

––. *The Constants of Nature*. New York: Pantheon Books, 2002.

Enz, Charles P. *No Time to be Brief: A Scientific Biography of Wolfgang Pauli*. New York: Oxford University Press, 2002.

Fisher, Nick. *Hybris: A Study in the Values of Honour and Shame in Ancient Greece*. Warminster: Aris & Phillips, 1992.

Gardner, Martin. *Science: Good, Bad and Bogus*. Buffalo, NY: Prometheus Books, 1981.

Gauquelin, Michel. *Cosmic Influences on Human Behavior*. Santa Fe, NM: Aurora Press, 1994.

Giannini, A. James, Joanne Daood, Matthew C. Giannini, Raymond Boniface and P. Gregg Rhodes. 'Intellect versus Intuition: A Dichotomy in the Reception of Nonverbal Communication.' *Journal of General Psychology*, 99:1 (July 1978), 19–24.

Herodotus. *The Histories*. Trans. George Rawlinson. Among other publishers, Everyman Library and Wordsworth Classic Edition.

Hesiod. *Theogony*. Available online at www.sacred-texts.com/cla/hesiod/theogony.htm

Homer. *The Iliad*. Trans. Richmond Lattimore. Chicago, IL: University of Chicago Press, 1951.

––. *The Odyssey*. Trans. Samuel Butler. Project Gutenberg edition, 1898. Available at www.gutenberg.org

Houdini, Harry. *Miracle Mongers and Their Methods: A Complete Exposé*. (1920). Amherst, NY: Prometheus Books (reprint edition), 1993.

Jolly, Karen, Catharina Raudvere and Edward Peters. *Witchcraft and Magic in Europe: The Middle Ages*. London: Athlone Press (Continuum Imprint), 2001.

Jung, Carl. *Psychological Types*. Vol. 6 of Bollingen Series XX. Princeton, NJ: Princeton University Press, 1971.

Kerényi, Karl. *The Gods of the Greeks*. London: Thames & Hudson, 1951.

Knoll, Andrew H. *Life on a Young Planet: The First Three Billion Years of Evolution on Earth*. Princeton, NJ: Princeton University Press, 2003.

Lemaitre, G. 'The Evolution of the Universe: Discussion'. *Nature*, 128: 3234 (24 October 1931), 699–701.

Lewis, C. S. *Miracles: A Preliminary Study*. New York: Macmillan and Co., 1947.

Lewis, David. *On the Plurality of Worlds*. Oxford: Blackwell, 1986.

Lucas, John Randolph. *A Treatise on Time and Space*. London: Metheun, 1973.

MacTaggart, J. M. E. 'The Unreality of Time'. *Mind*, XVII:4 (1908), 457–474.

Mercado, Rodrigo, Constantine Constantoyannis, Tornasz Mandat, Ajit Kumar, Michael Schulzer, A. John Stoessl and Christopher R. Honey. 'Expectation and the placebo effect in Parkinson's disease patients with sub thalamic nucleus deep brain stimulation'. *Movement Disorders*, 21:9 (September 2006), 1457–61.

Nostradamus' Index.

Peck, Harry Thurston. *Harpers Dictionary of Classical Antiquities.* (1898). Available online at various digital libraries including http://www.lib.uchicago.edu/efts/PERSEUS/Reference/harpers.html

Polkinghorne, John. *Faith, Science and Understanding.* New Haven, CT: Yale University Press, 2000.

Powell, James Laurence. *Mysteries of Terra Firma: The Age and Evolution of the Earth.* New York: Simon & Schuster, 2001.

Renault, Mary. *The Persian Boy.* [Alexander the Great]. London: Longmans, 1972.

Sagan, Carl. *The Demon-Haunted World: Science as a Candle in the Dark.* New York: Ballantine Books, 1996.

Schimmel, Annemarie. *The Mystery of Numbers.* Oxford: Oxford University Press, 1996.

Seymour, Dr. Percy. *Astrology: The Evidence of Science.* London: Penguin Group, 1988.

Shridhar, V. K. *Hindu Electional Astrology.* Haryana (India): Suvaas Publishers, 2002.

Smith, William. *Dictionary of Greek and Roman Biography and Mythology.* Published in 1870. London: I.B. Tauris, 2007.

Taylor, Stuart Ross. *Destiny or Chance: Our Solar System and Its Place in the Cosmos.* Cambridge: Cambridge University Press, 1998.

Tegmark, Max. 'Parallel Universes'. *Scientific American*, May 2003.

Teresi, Dick. *Lost Discoveries: The Ancient Roots of Modern Science – From the Babylonian to the Maya.* New York: Simon and Schuster, 2002.

Turcan, Robert. *The Cults of the Roman Empire.* Trans. by Antonia Nevill. Oxford: Blackwell, 1996.

Ussher, James. *The Annals of the World.* (1650). Republication, ed. by Larry and Marion Pierce. Green Forest, AR: Master Books.

Wang, Aihe. *Cosmology and Political Culture in Early China.* Cambridge: Cambridge University Press, 2000.

Ward, Peter D. and Donald Brownlee. *Rare Earth: Why Complex Life is Uncommon in the Universe.* New York: Copernicus Books (Springer-Verlag), 2000.

Webb, Stephen. *If the Universe is Teeming with Aliens – Where is Everybody? Fifty Solutions to the Fermi Paradox and the Problem of Extraterrestrial Life.* New York: Copernicus Books (Springer-Verlag), 2002.

Woodward, Kenneth L. *The Book of Miracles: The Meaning of the Miracle Stories in Christianity, Judaism, Buddhism, Hinduism and Islam.* New York: Simon and Schuster, 2000.

Internet references

'7 (un)Luckiest People in the World'. www.2spare.com/item_91685.aspx

'Agamemnon'. www.pantheon.org/articles/a/agamemnon.html

'Age of the Earth'. US Geological survey, 1997. http://pubs.usgs.gov/gip/geotime/age.html

'Astrology' in *The Dictionary of the History of Ideas* http://xtf.lib.virginia.edu/xtf/view?docId=DicHist/uvaBook/tei/DicHist1.xml

'Common Superstitions'. http://www.csicop.org/superstition/library/common.html

'Evidence for the Big Bang'. http://talkorigins.org/faqs/astronomy/bigbang.html

Hand, Robert. 'The History of Astrology: Another View'. www.arhatmedia.com/histintr.htm

Parry, Wynne. 'Brainless Jellyfish Navigates with Specialised Eyes'. www.LiveScience.com

Pinizzotto, Anthony J., Edward F. Davis and Charles E. Miller III. 'Emotional/rational decision making in law enforcement'. Free Online Library. www.thefreelibrary.com/Emotional%2Frational+decision+making+in+law+enforcement.-a0114370262

Stinnett, Tina Marie. 'What is Feng Shui?' www.fengshuifacts.org/

Chapter 8 Luck: How to Improve It

Armstrong, Karen. *Buddha.* London: Penguin Books, 2000.

Harvey, Peter. *An Introduction to Buddhism: Teaching, History and Practices.* Cambridge: Cambridge University Press, 1990.

James, William. *The Principles of Psychology.* 2 vols. Published in 1890. Mineola, NY: Dover Publications, 1950

Maslow, Abraham H. 'A Theory of Human Motivation'. *Psychological Review,* 50 (1943), 370–96.

––. *Motivation and Personality.* New York: Harper, 1954.

Meyer, Donald. *The Positive Thinkers.* New York: Pantheon Books, 1965.

Peale, Norman Vincent. *The Power of Positive Thinking.* Among other publishers, Cedar Books and Vermilion.

Internet references

'What Makes People Happy? The Top 10 List'. www.joyfuldays.com/what-makes-people-happy-the-top-10-list

www.theatlantic.com/magazine/archive/2009/06/what-makes-us-happy/307439/